GARDENS
& DEER

CHARLES COLES

GARDENS & DEER

A Guide to Damage Limitation

SWAN·HILL
PRESS

First Published in the UK in 1997
by Swan Hill Press, an imprint of Airlife Publishing Ltd

British Library Cataloguing-in-Publication Data
  A catalogue record for this book
  is available from the British Library

ISBN 1 85310 965 7

Typeset by Phoenix Typesetting, Ilkley, West Yorkshire.
Printed in England by St Edmundsbury Press Ltd, Bury St Edmunds, Suffolk.

Swan Hill Press

an imprint of Airlife Publishing Ltd
101 Longden Road, Shrewsbury, SY3 9EB, England.

ACKNOWLEDGEMENTS

My sincere thanks are due to the countless gardeners, who freely offered detailed observations on what deer were doing in their gardens: what they ate and what they avoided; the heights they jumped to gain entry; deterrents – successful and otherwise; trial techniques designed to minimise the damage and so on.

My postbag was full of variety, and perhaps I had not expected gardeners to have such literary talent! Whether it was about the roe drinking at the lily pool, some drama in the bluebell wood, or the devastation of a rose bed by muntjac, everything was described with eloquence and wit. The mix of lyricism, rage or humour, that often accompanied the down-to-earth recordings of deer behaviour, made a job that was often frustrating into one that was always fascinating.

Additional information came from scientists, deer consultants, gamekeepers, foresters, fencing contractors and others – at home and abroad – whom I contacted on matters that required their special expertise. From the USA, Bob Tanem, a director of a Garden Center in California, kindly sent me his 'Deer Resistant Planting', which provided a great deal of data relevant to UK conditions, for which I am grateful. In his report, covering thirty years of observations on deer in gardens, he says: 'This is intended to be a starting point for a landscaping in a heavy deer population area'.

My book is just that – a starting point.

The distribution maps of the different deer species, were prepared by the Biological Records Centre, ITE, Monks Wood, from data supplied by the British Deer Society and the Mammal Society, using DMAP mapping software written by Dr A. Morton, and are included by courtesy of ITE.

The press were very co-operative in helping to get the project off the ground: in particular *The Field, BBC Gardeners' World, Gardening WHICH, Home and Country*, (Women's Institute), *The Game Conservancy Magazine, Deer* (British Deer Society), a CLA Newsletter and many provincial newspapers.

My wife also deserves special thanks for allowing – albeit grudgingly – the local fallow deer into our garden for 'observation purposes', when I granted them a three-year truce.

With few exceptions, I have not mentioned by name any of those who contributed to the investigation, as I felt it might have involved them in a great deal of correspondence, which they might not have had the time to deal with.

Photographs unless indicated otherwise are by the author.

CHARLES COLES

CONTENTS

INTRODUCTION

Setting up an Investigation

In the early days I tried – and failed – to get various official bodies to finance a modest study of the problem of deer raiding gardens. I think it was the word 'gardens' that probably made them baulk at the idea. Damage to farm and forest crops was worthy of serious attention, but our rose beds and runner beans were of minor importance. The other reason was no doubt that the problem was considered to be insoluble. The author of the rather limited RHS list of deer-resistant plants had wisely commented that there had been a lot of conflicting evidence in the survey. Other experts had said the same thing – that nothing could be guaranteed as absolutely deer-proof. However, I was aware of this before I started: the unpredictability and eccentric feeding habits of deer are well-known.

The professionally maintained gardens that are open to the public are usually protected by deer-proof fences – in some cases a ha-ha – so they have no worries. On the whole, neither do the large country estates. When I asked landowner friends how they coped, they invariably said, 'Just manage your deer population correctly; erect 7 ft fencing, if necessary, and you will have no trouble'. The advice is perfectly sound, but not practicable for the average amateur living at Jasmine Cottage or the Old Vicarage.

Gathering Some Basic Facts

Having decided to go it alone, I wrote to a number of country magazines and gardening journals, and asked readers for lists of so-called deer-resistant plants, with any back-up information that might be relevant, i.e. the species of deer concerned, the time of the year when the damage was at its worst, the presence of any dogs, security lights, cattle grids, special fences, the use of deterrents and so on.

I also asked for lists of plants that were especially palatable to deer and regularly eaten down. While everyone knows that roses and pansies are at the top of the highly vulnerable list, there are also a large number of lesser known plants that are equally at risk. Losing them could be costly. The same applied to the survivors: a patch of London pride or some self-sown nasturtiums could easily be ignored and escape comment. I wanted the lists to be as comprehensive as possible.

There are also all the 'in-between' plants which are sometimes eaten, sometimes not. For them it is useful to have all possible explanations and observations, however insignificant they might seem. For example: 'That was the year our neighbour put sheep in the field next door and the deer ceased to visit us'. And so on.

Those who replied to my questions did so enthusiastically. In addition to information on the palatability or otherwise of the various plants, information was also forthcoming on those that were toxic, edible to humans, had medical or even aphrodisiac properties, kept witches away, could be dried for decorative purposes, smelled objectionable indoors, were slug- or rabbit-proof, or had some historical significance! There was a touch of the mediaeval herbalist about some of the comments. And there were often personal asides, such as: 'I have another mole messing up the lawn'. In due course, I began to feel I knew that lawn and its moles.

Some of the side-issues were fascinating as well as informative. For instance, with regard to crocuses, a flower that has puzzled me greatly, it seems that the yellow ones are invariably eaten before the mauve ones. There were many reports on this issue. Also that sparrows have been seen attacking them furiously: again, the yellow ones being the most popular. Rabbits have also been seen eating them, pheasants caught red-handed, Thames-side mallard – also slugs – and squirrels are suspected of digging up the bulbs. A friend in Sweden, a deer expert, tells me 'Roe seem to avoid yellow flowers such as yellow crocus . . .', so perhaps most of our crocus damage is not due to deer, but primarily to sparrows etc? Years ago I recall an old biologist friend of mine, who was a keen gardener, telling me that voles (or was it long-tailed fieldmice?) were eating his crocus bulbs but selecting only one colour. However, I cannot now remember which colour, and my old friend has long since died.

Reports on deer in gardens came in from the USA and Canada, where many of the same problems were encountered – an expatriate even wrote in from Brazil. I also consulted colleagues with technical knowledge in some of the fringe areas, who were working in Austria, Belgium, France, Germany, Portugal and Sweden, though most of these countries suffer little garden damage by comparison.

The level of expertise varied considerably, as did the spelling of fuchsia! Some of those who knew about deer were often rather shaky on their gardening, and many of the experienced gardeners couldn't recognise one deer species from another: 'They're just deer – some have horns and others do not'. Or the deer were nocturnal and came and went unseen. One troubled gardener told his neighbour to look out for a 'large spotted rabbit', which turned out to be a roe deer kid!

Detective work was sometimes needed to clarify which plants were really involved. Syringa popped up as philadelphus or mock orange, whereas it is, of course, lilac. And 'geraniums' caused confusion. Did the writer mean the perennial variety (cranesbills), or the pelargonium which most of us have called a geranium since we first bought one for a windowsill?

Once on the telephone I asked about '*Myosotis*'.

'My what?' she queried.

'*M Y O S O T I S*' I said.

'Oh, you mean forget-me-not'. Clearly my fault.

And when someone wrote 'My viburnums are eaten', and there are 150 varieties listed in the RHS Plant Finder – some of which are decimated while others are ignored – how should I proceed? With some plants like azaleas, there are both deciduous and evergreen varieties which needed some identifying: the deer had preferences. With others, like heathers, it was whether they were summer-flowering or winter-flowering that made a difference. Generalisations could in some cases be misleading.

The majority of my correspondents were ladies (66% in fact) and letters were often signed 'fellow sufferer' and contained messages of sympathy. The co-operation was heart-warming. I was left wondering whether nice people take to gardening or whether gardening makes people nice. I feel the same about country postmen.

A most helpful lady from Scotland apologised for not being able to identify certain plants, because soon after planting them she bought a 'West Highland terrorist puppy, which delighted in removing all the labels and hiding them in a nest under one of the larch trees'.

Among the correspondents there were many experts who gave the plant names in Latin as well, so that there could be no confusion. But some muddle there will always be, as botanists and taxonomists continue to re-classify plants, and their synonyms prosper like weeds. Seed catalogues and garden centres often use different names to those in plant encyclopaedias.

At the start of the survey I had planned to publish just the basic lists of plants eaten or ignored by deer, which could have been issued as a fairly compact and inexpensive bulletin. However, the more I got involved in the problem, the more complex I found it to be, and the more I realised that many of the plants described could not be put tidily into one category or the other without explanations. I also wanted to try and deal with some of the points that had been raised from time to time when I walked round plundered gardens with their disillusioned owners. So many questions cannot be answered by a simple yes or no, and unfortunately some will probably never be answered at all. The dining habits of deer remain an enigma. Finally, I felt that I couldn't waste the peripheral information and the colourful anecdotes so freely related to me. A selection have been included, and the original reference book has thus gone into a conversational mode. For those who simply want to know whether, say, Euphorbia is eaten or not, turn straight to the alphabetical list and read the distilled views – albeit sometimes divergent – of the many gardeners who contributed to this survey.

CHAPTER ONE

SOME ASPECTS OF THE PROBLEM

My involvement

I have lived on the edge of the New Forest for over thirty years, in harmony with such deer as crossed my path. But a few years ago increasing numbers of fallow started to invade my garden, and so began the destruction or mutilation of most of my plants and shrubs. It was this that prompted me to harness the expertise and goodwill of long-suffering gardeners and find out if anything could be done about it. I embarked on a two-year investigation, which eventually stretched to three.

Damage to woodlands had been studied very thoroughly by foresters and game biologists on an international basis for over a century or more. A survey of damage by deer to *gardens* would be breaking new ground.

What actually triggered off the project was the demolition of four newly acquired camellias, costing £15 each! In a few short visits they had been seriously trimmed back. By the second season, two were clearly dying and the other two reduced to a sort of bonsai shape. Simultaneously, long-established camellias that had never been touched before, were now being cropped up to nose height. By the ferocity of the attack, I assumed that camellias were probably next to roses in the palatability tables. I was quite wrong. In other gardens, in other areas, camellias are never touched!

Clearly there was a great deal to be investigated.

My curiosity was further aroused when I noticed that in a lot of unfenced gardens nearby, there were a number of shrub mallows (*lavatera*) which were growing well – untouched by roaming deer.

13

Accordingly, I bought three or four plants. All went well for a season or two, until a young buck started to visit the garden. In no time he had mowed down the *lavatera* and evidently taught other members of his tribe that they were edible. Eventually all the plants died.

As with camellias, mallows are *not* universally eaten down elsewhere.

As I have said, I knew before I started that deer had quirky tastes, and were unpredictable, capricious and opportunistic feeders. In many ways there was no logic to their feeding habits. Plant X would be eaten in one garden, and the same plant left alone in another. There were also individual 'rogues' who – when removed from the scene – allowed the vulnerable plant or plants to thrive again. And there were nibblers, and 'try-anything-oncers', and those who indulged in the 'flavour of the month' syndrome. Certainly, their favourites – like roses – never varied: nor did their rejects such as lavender.

I foresaw a number of problems, and met more than a few surprises on the way. As well as drawing on the experiences of fellow sufferers, I decided to use my one-acre garden as a test-bed or field laboratory. Instead of continually trying to scare away the deer, I would allow them free access to the property, so that I could observe their feeding behaviour and menu preferences at close quarters for the duration of the project.

The start of deer raids on gardens

Across the country it seemed that the trouble had only become serious in the last six or seven years. Extracts from letters included:

> 'Fallow and roe have been evident for the past twenty years, but over the last six they have become a PEST!' (Sussex)
>
> 'The last few years have seen a population explosion of roe, and no garden seems safe'. (Inverness-shire)
>
> 'We have been visited by fallow for the past eight or nine years, and they have done a lot of damage – even taking flowers from under our windows'. (Essex)
>
> 'We have always had roe deer in the neighbourhood, but they rarely caused any problems until 1993, when numerous species of plants were devoured nightly'. (Dorset)

14

In my own case, we rarely saw any deer in the garden or in the surrounding fields until six or seven years ago. If we glimpsed a deer on our forest walks it would be quite an event. The increase in their numbers and the invasion of gardens has been a fairly recent phenomenon and the culling has not been able to keep pace with it.

The same huge increase in deer numbers has recently been reported in Sweden, though some of this has been attributed to the present low level of foxes, killed off by various diseases such as mange, scabies etc. The foxes were severe predators on roe kids. A similar disregard of humans has been apparent. The USA has the same problem, reported Alistair Cooke recently in his *Letter from America*. He added that very few State Governors or City Mayors would dare to offend voters by instituting any noticeable control – or words to that effect.

Culling considered

Culling is, of course, only part of a complex overall management strategy – the basic aim being to limit the deer numbers to the habitat available, or in some cases to re-think the forest design, or both. If this is not done, the deer lose condition, sometimes die, and in an effort to find fresh sources of food they can create an unacceptable amount of damage in any new-found territory. Gardens are among the areas that suffer most.

A comment from Surrey makes the point: 'Here the deer have increased in numbers in the last ten years and are now unable to sustain themselves in the quite extensive heathland and woods of this area, and are a PLAGUE – visiting gardens by day and night, having to be kept out only by high and unsightly fencing. Clearly, there is a need for careful culling of the animals, but I have no idea where the responsibility for such action lies'.

There are about one million deer in the country at the present and they are still increasing. 'The deer population has reached crisis levels . . .' wrote an expert in January 1995. To some extent the rise in numbers follows the expansion of afforestation, and the fact that deer have now adapted to living in cover that they would have judged unsuitable some years ago.

By deer, five species are meant: red, roe, fallow, sika and muntjac.

(I am omitting the little Chinese water deer – reportedly used as the Babycham symbol – which is really an escapee from wildlife parks, and only found in a few pockets in the country).

As far as the responsibility for deer damage is concerned, several unhappy gardeners have written to me saying the same thing – that no authority seems to be accountable for the control of deer, and so literally 'the buck is passed'. One puzzled country-man – on being told by the local environmental department that it was certainly not their responsibility, asked about shooting them and enjoying some venison. 'They were aghast!' he reported. Another sufferer – hoping for some help with damage limitation – approached his local council, the police, the National Trust and the bursar of a neighbouring school – both the latter were pro-viding shelter for the roe. After some deliberation, the council offered to put up a couple of roadsigns saying 'CAUTION DEER'. Clearly in some areas the nature of the problem is not really understood!

Where there is no local authority to render assistance, nearby landowners, timber growers and others, who may be providing some of the cover for the raiding deer, are usually willing to help and may have gamekeepers or rangers who will undertake culling during the open season. This varies according to the different species, and the sex of the animals.

A local estate owner who was manfully battling with deer control commented that, 'They are rather like the Zulus, in that every time you shoot one, another instantly appears to take its place!' Unoccupied territories soon fill up. Unfortunately, deer are now living on the edges of residential areas, the fringe of golf courses, in the grounds of large country hotels – even in a large crematorium garden, so a friend tells me.

This unlikely habitat reminds me of a day when I was shooting driven pheasants in Hampshire, and the keeper placed me in the churchyard, which was part of the estate concerned. 'They do come over the church roof lovely,' he said. I suppose I looked slightly wor-ried at the thought of letting off my gun, while standing amid the tombstones, but the keeper reassured me, 'Do you shoot away, Sir. They won't 'ear yer!' I did as I was bid.

In some rural areas where there are no keepers who might be able to help with the culling, there may be a highly qualified 'deer controller' who can come to the rescue, though it is unlikely that he will be able to do very much in some leafy suburb, which may be nurturing a coven of small secretive muntjac.

Deer control can take many forms. From the USA a Press article reported that: 'a doe had crashed through the window of the ladies' lounge at the National Institute of Standards and Technology in Maryland. Then the deer ate all the wild flowers in the Institute's stately grounds. Finally – and this was the last straw – they started eating the Institute's azaleas. Now the *Washington Times* tells us that the NIST is employing the Humane Society to fire darts 'primed with a contraceptive' through blowpipes. The Institute hoped that this would reduce the size of the herd and so protect the azaleas'. Other more dramatic methods had first been considered, including that of unleashing a pack of wolves on the estate. 'But the concensus was,' an official said 'that, while we might lose a few deer, we might also lose a few slow-moving chemists and engineers.'

Where culling is impossible for one reason or another, the gardener will have to go on the defensive. Basically, this involves growing fewer plants that tempt the deer, and more that they find unpalatable. It may be heartbreaking to grass over the rose beds and perhaps some of the herbaceous borders, but it is surprising how may colourful plants there are that the deer will leave alone. This strategy, as well as various protective measures, is discussed in later chapters.

The economic value of deer – outside the garden

It should be remembered that deer have a value: they are an impor-tant natural resource, both in our forests and on our wild uplands. The latter can produce little else in the way of income other than from sheep, some cattle grazing, grouse shooting and deer-stalking.

At one time the deer in our forests were considered largely as pests – like grey squirrels and rabbits. They damaged trees and were dealt with accordingly. By contrast, on the Continent the foresters had for generations also been trained as game rangers, and the deer were managed with great expertise. Damage to timber crops was kept to a minimum, and a good secondary revenue was generated by letting the deer-stalking to approved hunters. Now we have long since caught up with the hunting and game management skills of the European foresters. Indeed, many foreign sportsmen come to Britain for first class stalking. Good trophies can earn a lot of money, over a £1,000 for a gold medal head, and the production of venison is not unimportant. If however, you asked a Head Forester whether his roe deer ate pansies or pinks, he might not know. Bluebells or coppiced hazel shoots? Yes!

Deer lose their fear of man

In addition to the increase in numbers, deer in many areas, such as the New Forest, have changed their habits. They have largely lost their fear of humans, having been exposed to the comings and goings of ramblers, riders, dog walkers, cyclists, campers, caravanners and others, in what were once wild and remote refuges. Elsewhere, even in suburbia, deer have abandoned their reclusive sylvan ways. They now enter our gardens nonchalantly in broad daylight, eating roses off the front of our houses in the early hours. Flowers, such as winter pansies in patio tubs, are grazed to soil level, as well as pelargoniums growing in pots within a few feet of buildings – and in some cases in window boxes. Dogs and security lights make little difference.

One lady wrote to say that she meets the deer walking calmly in through the front gate when she catches the early train to London. Another, that they have a nodding acquaintance with the 5 a.m. milkman; and from the West Country came two reports that red deer had been eating the flowers from graves – in one case with a group of nonplussed ladies attending to their weekly tidying-up duties. Elsewhere, roe and muntjac have also been observed doing this.

From Winchester, a correspondent wrote: 'Last summer I walked through the arch into the precinct of the Cathedral, and standing in the middle of a grassy patch opposite the Deanery was a roe deer grazing the herbage; it looked very contented – other passers-by had not noticed it'. When discussing the fairly common problem of rabbits eating flowers on graves, I was told of a spaniel who always embarrassed its owner by retrieving any wreaths, when being walked through the churchyard! Another described a wandering sheep making a bee-line for a Christmas wreath of red-berried holly that he had just laid on his grandparents' grave. It had totally ignored another holly bush en route, which had no berries. Sheep will also eat flowers on graves, and have to be excluded, which can be as difficult as it is with deer. Finally on the churchyard theme, I recently heard that on the day after the funeral of an old friend of mine, Prince Heinrich Reuss of Austria – a lifelong hunter and student of game – red deer were seen in the village churchyard eating the fresh flowers that had been placed on his grave. How he would have loved that!

Other comments from contributors regarding the increased audacity of deer include:

> 'The roe sometimes come up and stare at us through the windows, and we can see their shiny wet noses clearly – they are that close'.
> 'Our fallow sometimes lie down on our lawn, close to the house – like cows in a meadow'.
> 'The fallow walk down the main street in the early mornings and eat the pansies etc from outside the front door.'
> 'Fallow droppings were found inside the porch of a house where there was something very edible in the garden'.
> 'The fallow even rub their noses on my kitchen window. I get up to twenty at a time on my lawn in winter, and where they walk is almost like a ploughed field'.
> 'Here the roe are very tame and will stand eating my water lilies – even though I may be only a few yards away, and my dogs giving tongue'.
> 'The roe seem to be more brazen than they used to be, and often stand in our field and glare at us as we walk round our garden – reluctant to moved even when we make noises'.
> 'The muntjac are shameless and do not withdraw even when approached. They are to be seen at night and during the day. At night they wander freely around our unlit village. The actual damage happens during the hours of darkness'.

The *National Geographic* magazine wrote: 'White-tailed deer are creatures of ineffable grace and beauty, with delicacy and strength, and an uncanny way of disappearing into deep foliage. Their elegance, though, is belied by a voracious appetite, and they easily get used to humans'.

And from many sources come reports that deer are not in the least bothered by heavy traffic. I do not think this is the same reaction as when deer wander across a road at night and sometimes get killed. Deer now seem to be acclimatised to the aural and visual disturbance of nearby motor vehicles. A local ranger has seen them mating a few yards from the road, with the cars thundering past at night in a blaze of headlights.

Once conditioned, these garden-dwelling deer seem to adapt to the presence of humans more or less permanently. On the open hills of the North their behaviour is different. During the stalking season the stags are watchful and wary; therein lies the fascination of the hunt – perhaps hours of crawling on one's stomach to get within range. But ten days after the end of the stalking season, on many estates the wild stags will recognise the approach of the truck with potatoes for their winter feeding and practically gallop down to meet it. However, when some months later the truce is over, the same deer will once again become suspicious at the faintest scent or merest whisper of a human. Garden deer do not seem to revert, though they may react briefly when an owner buys a new car, or something of the sort.

My own experience regarding our local fallow confirms all the reports that have come in. In bright sunlight they will walk around the house, taking a nibble here and a nibble there, though always on the alert. They never relax their wariness, and will stop eating in mid-nibble if they think they hear some sound that is unfamiliar. Their radar ears are working all the time. But the noise of the radio, lavatories flushing, the central-heating engine running, the dishwasher in action do not disturb them. Occasionally, voices do, and in our house, the sound of the carriage clock chiming through an open window on a quiet evening.

If I disturb them when they are eating their favourite windfall apples, they will run resentfully into nearby cover but return to their feasting within minutes. They adapt quite quickly to unfamiliar objects such as colourful washing on the line, new garden furniture, a croquet set and so on. Deer that visit the same garden regularly get used to almost anything that confronts them. They also bring in hangers-on who rapidly lose any initial fear they may have, because they are accompanied by the old hands who move about confidently.

Last November a large buck, a newcomer, appeared within twenty yards of the house and started to gobble up some fallen apples. He had, I am sure, been invited by our regular visitors, who were not far away. I doubt that he would have wandered in from the forest on his own in broad daylight, and settled down to feed so close by, unless he had been following the scent of a female and happened upon the irresistible apples.

Quite recently some fallow resolutely munched their way through trays of young polyanthus plants ready for sale, just inside the opening of a polythene tunnel owned by the local nurseryman. They also reached in for some early beans.

Their attitude to humans has undoubtedly changed. I cannot think that ten years ago a retired Naval Commander, living near Brockenhurst, would have told me that the roe sometimes stood outside the window intently watching him writing at his desk, and, as he put it, 'seeming quite curious about what I was actually putting down on paper'. But he hadn't thought it sufficiently odd to write to the *Field* about it. None of their antics surprised him any more.

To keep things in perspective, as well as the deer with the new audacious spirit, there are equally reports of furtive, unseen deer, often muntjac but sometimes roe, raiding gardens at night or in the very early hours. Unfortunately, the fallow around our village patrol the gardens day and night. One moonlit night, we watched a white doe browsing among the shadowy trees; it was beautiful and rather eerie. On dark nights I often hear rustling noises, and aim a powerful torch at the sound. Pairs of very bright eyes shine back intently; the animals seem transfixed and rarely move while the beam is on them. Arthur Cadman, one-time Deputy Surveyor of the New Forest, recounts how one of his keepers caught a fallow buck in the glare of his headlights, and while the animal was immobilised by the beam, walked quietly up to him and put his hat on its antlers. Moving or strobing lights, however, usually cause panic reactions.

Attitudes to deer in gardens

A number of gardeners not only described the destruction of their valued plants but also their protection ploys and their many disappointments in trying to cope with the raiding deer. Also described were their individual feelings about these contrary creatures – beautiful, but determined marauders. Exasperation could follow admiration, and vice versa. This I understood profoundly. I had experienced the latter when watching the white doe at close quarters feeding in the moonlight. She did not know that she was being observed, and this added to the drama: it was theatrical.

It would be indulgent to describe the many varied experiences of my chance contacts with deer, that have left me with a feeling of awe, but one in particular has stayed with me in sharp focus as though it happened yesterday, instead of thirty years ago. I had stumbled across a tiny spotted roe kid – only a few hours old – that had fallen into a drainage ditch on a lonely Scottish moor. The innocent frightened eyes invited every cliché in the book.

One moment you are privileged to be sharing a deer's secrets, and the next – perhaps after every single rose bloom has again been bitten off – you are feeling like reaching for your rifle. I felt a great deal of sympathy for two different ladies who open their gardens to the public once a year for charity. In both cases a day or two before the event, with all the invitations sent out and the notices up, the deer got in and laid waste the gardens.

Some specimen reactions to visiting deer include the following:

Welcome visitors
'They are welcome in my garden. The sight of a fawn basking in the summer sun beneath the washing line is compensation enough for the loss of a year's runner beans. . .' (Ed. Clearly a very tolerant lady as she had also lost all her grape hyacinths, and a 'massed bank of spring bulbs'. Her rambler roses had also been 'pruned'.) From the *WI Journal.*

Disillusionment
'We smile to ourselves when we remember how thrilled we were when we first saw roe deer in the field at the back of the property. Little did we know what we had in store!' (Hampshire)

'Ironically enough it was the sight of a deer parading across the bottom of this long garden on the day we first came to view the house that persuaded us that we must buy it. That, of course, was before we realised how much damage they can do, and before I spent a considerable amount of money on expensive plants to feed them with'. (Bucks)

'The muntjac proved too much for us . . . the novelty of these inquisitive little creatures ferreting in the borders soon wore thin. An all-round 5 ft fence was eventually erected'. (Herts)

Mixed emotions
'We were happy for the muntjac to feed on food put out for the birds, but when the snow melted, they devoured all the irises, crocuses, tulips . . .' (Suffolk)

More culling needed
'The fallow bother all the neighbours around here and are a plaguey nuisance: too many of them – there needs to be a cull'. (Hampshire)

(And a great many other correspondents demanding similar action – Ed).

Distinctly anti-deer
'We have all but given up trying to grow herbaceous plants here . . . roe deer are our Number One enemy – we do not regard them as dear little "Bambis", but as pernicious pests'. (Hampshire)

'I spent £15 on winter pansies last Christmas and the muntjac and fallow demolished the lot. What I call these deer is nobody's business. People riding round in cars see them in fields, stop and take photos of them, and say how lovely they are – but not me! I am *infested* with deer . . . I've had to give over nearly all my garden to grass, because everything is eaten off, and what they don't eat, they urinate on – so the plants die'. (Essex)

'Have had to spend over £1,500 on chain-link fencing to keep muntjac out of our one-acre garden'. (East Anglia)

And too many to quote who have sadly had to dig up or grass over lovely rose beds that they have tended for years.

The majority view
Typical extracts include:

'They increase every year and need to be reduced, and though I

23

love to see them – roe and fallow – I naturally prefer them in the forest and NOT where I am trying to garden'. (Hampshire)

'I love to watch them on the *other* side of the fence'. (Berkshire)

'We have roe deer, which are lovely to watch, as long as they aren't in *our* garden or woods'. (Lancs)

In other words: 'NOT in my backyard!' By far the greatest number of reports (57%) about damage to gardens were concerned with roe deer. But for some reason the species that attracted the most opprobrium was the muntjac. Perhaps because it is so sneakily successful at wrecking a garden?

CHAPTER TWO

THE MAIN TRIALS AREA

The above is a rather overblown description of my one-acre garden on the edge of the New Forest, which I used as a test-bed for the project. It required a considerable degree of self control to allow the deer into our garden 'without let or hindrance'. But throughout the three years I succeeded in living at close quarters with the deer and learned a great deal. Inevitably, a love-hate relationship developed.

When they visited the garden – which at certain periods of the year was every day – I recorded numbers, approximate ages, sex, what they were eating, any fraying damage and general activities. I could often recognise some of the regulars, because of their individual features. At one time we had a white doe and later a chocolate coloured fawn among the visitors, who were prospecting from their home coverts four-and-a-half miles away. A mother and her young were practically always with us throughout the summer, and we got to know their behaviour pattern. Occasionally, a strange three- or four-year-old buck would appear, and we would notice that following his arrival quite different plants would be eaten – plants that had not hitherto been touched. Unfortunately, the regulars would often learn from his particular menu preferences: the damage would increase and continue after he had moved on.

From our upstairs windows I could virtually see into every corner of the garden. In addition to these sightings I undertook a daily tour of the property, tracking the intruders' movements during the previous night, or the very early hours. Fresh droppings, slot marks, trampled plants, newly eaten flowers, nibbled shoots, bitten off and discarded items and so on, made this quite easy. I also logged the weather conditions, which had a bearing on what they were eating.

To assist in the garden I was lucky enough to have someone – born and bred in the Forest – whose main job as a fencing contractor took him all over the surrounding countryside, and every week we compared notes on the deer's activities: where the various herds had gone, whether the rut had started, what the animals were feeding on in other gardens and so on. His report often helped me to put in place another piece of my one-acre jigsaw puzzle. And quite often I was out in the Forest myself, visiting other gardens in the neighbourhood.

There is little point in describing the garden in any detail, but a few general remarks may be relevant. About a quarter of the garden consists of untended wilderness, interspersed with old fruit trees, silver birch, holly, laurels, briars, honeysuckle and ivy – the latter eaten everywhere to nose height. Ivy is a useful standby winter food. This area provides welcome cover for the deer at all times of the year. We have two fairly large lawns, with more moss than grass. Until the deer invasion we had a number of colourful flower beds, but we had to grass over about half of them, and in the remainder we have gradually been discarding the more palatable plants and replacing them with the more resistant ones. Our only roses now are the climbers against the walls of the house, with the usual bare stems at the base, screened where possible by other shrubs. We also have a huge Himalayan musk, which is protected all round by a thick skirt of mature rhododendrons; and a runaway pink *raubritter*, which has climbed up a tall apple tree. This is protected at the base by a tangle of berberis, and the lily pool, with its one portly, heron-proof goldfish. One summer we watched two slim young grass snakes clearing the pond of tadpoles: not one was left! Elsewhere, deer have been seen wading in to eat water lily buds and blooms, but we have so far had no trouble. Flag irises survive.

Dotted about our garden there are a number of trees, including a magnificent copper beech, some laburnums, an old magnolia and several shrubs and plants ignored by the deer, such as buddleia, weigela, skimmia, mahonia, catmint, golden oregano, senecio 'Silver dust', pineapple mint and other herbs, to list only a small selection. In the spring the whole place is ablaze with snowdrops, wild daffodils, bluebells – heavily grazed, but surviving – and untouched primroses. We have narcissi in beds and tubs, but no tulips or hyacinths, which are real deer fodder. Later we grew mixed tulips and wallflowers in tubs, behind unobtrusive green netting. It's not quite the garden we would choose – now with more shrubs than flowers – but it is improving gradually as we learn how to adapt.

26

Such vegetables we grow are in a safe, screened-off area, which was here when we came thirty years ago. In this protected zone I have some roses grown for cutting – and sweet peas – which climb up the indispensable runner beans. At least, if we cannot have rose beds to admire, we can have vases of roses and sweet peas in the house, to remind us that we still are gardeners – of a sort. In an old unheated greenhouse, we grow a succession of sweet scented lilies in terracotta pots, which are moved out onto a terrace, as they come into flower. In front of them is a screen of smaller plants in various containers. These include foliage plants, such as *helichrysums* and other inedible greenery. Inquisitive animals will occasionally lean over and nip off a lily bud, but not very often. Lilies planted in beds tend to get eaten off when they are about 18 in high, or have their centres bitten out. We find it useful to keep a few single lilies in 'sink-able' pots, which we can slip into any beds that have been ravaged. When they are in bud they are usually safe. Day lilies are, of course, a non-starter in most gardens. Now and again, I buy a few 'test plants', usually as a result of someone telling me that 'deer never eat my so-and-sos'. Sometimes they remain untouched, but the curiosity factor of the animals can ruin the experiment – particularly if I put in only one or two plants – and they get snapped up. But I have confirmed the inedibility of a number of doubtful plants by this method.

The main playground for the deer is at the back of the house, where there are quite a few apple trees, grandly referred to as the 'orchard'. The nearest tree is only a dozen yards from the kitchen window, and in the late summer when there are plenty of windfalls on the ground, we often see two or three deer guzzling them up avidly. Their table manners are atrocious! Their mouths froth with juice, and bits of peel fall to the ground as they chomp. Not content with eating apples on the ground they sometimes stand on their back legs, take a few wobbly steps as though on stilts and pick fruit off the trees or knock them down. It is wonderful entertainment, and makes the love-hate relationship more understandable.

Last autumn I hung up some apples on string to see if they would have a go at bobbing for them. For a short while they were a little suspicious, then an adult tried to grab one but much to her irritation it kept swinging away. In due course, she mastered the art and bit them off the string. Her young fawn watched this performance with some frustration because when it came to her turn, she found the apples were too big to seize in her mouth and they kept bopping her on the nose.

Beyond the fruit trees the ground rises up to the boundary fence some fifty yards away. This is the untended wilderness referred to earlier, which has to make do with a strimmer haircut once a year. Here there are quite a few peonies that look after themselves, as do clumps of Solomon's seal, the uninvited montbretia – which I must now learn to call *Crocosmia* – and some very welcome amaryllis belladonna lilies, which suffered some serious leaf-stripping during the drought, but are normally never touched. This area is nearly the 'wild woodland garden' of the glossy magazine writers, but not quite – there is no wooden seat. It is closer to Gerard Manley Hopkins's: 'What would the world be, once bereft of wet and wilderness? . . . long live the weeds and the wilderness yet.' There is plenty of that.

At the top of the slope under some laurels, the deer have made their 'lodge', where they often lie down and sometimes nod off . . . waking up to have a little scratch . . . to stretch their legs, and sometimes to watch us watching them. I have a feeling they are interested in what they can see through the kitchen windows . . . we are washing up, we are beating eggs with a whisk, we have switched on the radio. But I must not risk adopting Bambi sentiments.

One faithful correspondent – as yet none too familiar with the ways of the deer in her garden – wrote in a state of great pique that she had found what she described as some 'nests'. 'I believe they are now actually *sleeping* in our garden!' she wrote. Clearly, that was going too far.

The surrounding land

When frightened, the deer can easily slip out of the garden into a nearby thicket of gorse, thorn and bracken, or into a neighbouring grass field, where there is only an elderly horse, a fox earth and at most times of the year a great number of rabbits. They know their escape routes and never feel trapped. In this field I recently counted thrity-three fallow deer grazing peacefully in the afternoon sun. This sort of pressure causes great resentment to the owners of ponies or farm stock, who need the grass for their own animals.

Our property is in a 'hungry' area, which means that the plants in our green and regularly-watered garden are more likely to be devoured than those in gardens surrounded by well-farmed land, with cereals, root crops, and fertilised leys. The forest land all around us consists mostly of open heath, with the usual scattered scrub cover. It is nearly always overstocked with ponies, free ranging cattle belonging to the commoners, donkeys, a heavy deer population and vast numbers of rabbits. The grazing on any enclosed fields is inclined to be rather poor, the soil being thin and acid.

Houses tend to be somewhat isolated, so each garden can be a tempting oasis. This means that the visiting deer are more likely to eat plants on the borderline of palatability, than they would in richer, more verdant habitat, with a lower population of grazing and browsing animals. In other words, if a plant escapes destruction in my garden, it really must be unappetising, and as a trials area it provides an unusually severe testing ground.

As to other wildlife that share our territory, we have an extensive badger sett at the front gate, but they do not interact with deer. They scratch holes in the lawns for worms, and they dig up tulips and sometimes lily bulbs. There is also the fox earth in the neighbouring field, which means cubs in our gardens at frequent intervals. They do not take much notice of the deer or vice versa. They drink from the lily pool and sunbathe on the lawn, waking up from time to time to scratch fleas or to play games. We tolerate then as assistant rabbit catchers. For some years now, we have not had any dogs, and there are no security lights. But as explained elsewhere, in most circumstances, these make very little difference to the infiltrating deer.

My regular observations over the three-year period have taught me a great deal about the attitudes of deer to gardens and gardeners. Although we lived almost cheek-by-jowl with the deer, our regular visitors never became tame. Though much less frightened of us humans than were their ancestors, they remained wild creatures. I suspect that the regular doe, her fawn and the travelling companion (perhaps last year's young?) tolerated us as just a couple of strange mammals – with somewhat eccentric habits – who were sharing the same territory. The many other deer who passed through from time to time – staying a few days if there were any tempting food items – were perhaps a little more jumpy, but they would equally visit the garden in broad daylight, and within a day or two show little concern over 'unnatural' objects like parked cars, lawn mowers or brightly-coloured washing on the line.

Many other gardeners have written about their visiting roe families: their regular foraging routes, their particular likes and dislikes, and their individual habits in a garden. Several observers described how their roe practically always went browsing along the same track or in a set pattern, and this perhaps explains why normally tempting items that were off the usual route never got eaten.

'She knows exactly what she wants and goes straight for it', said one lady gardener. But this is too trusting: their perambulations can be as unpredictable as their dietary preferences. And one day the hitherto safe row of beans behind the privet hedge could be stripped.

CHAPTER THREE

THE DIFFERENT DEER SPECIES

How to recognise them

Rather than just having 'deer' in the garden, it is probably useful to know which species they are. They all have somewhat different habits. As there are several excellent books on deer giving detailed descriptions of all the species, I intend to take some short cuts and only touch on the basic differences. The illustrations of the males (stags/bucks) showing their varied antler formations should make recognition quite clear.

It is much harder to describe the females (hinds/does) who, of course, have no antlers. If you see a head and shoulders peering out of some bracken in the half light, one female face looks much like another. And even if the deer watcher has tables of weights and heights-at-the-shoulder, recognition is not that easy. The tight-skinned little muntjac, which probably doesn't resemble what the average person thinks a deer should look like, may be the exception.

For the average gardener – to keep it simple – either ask an experienced 'local' which deer are to be found in the neighbour-hood, or wait until an antlered male puts in an appearance, remembering that at certain seasons they cast their antlers. They grow new ones every year. The deer distribution maps should also help to show what species are likely to be in each area.

Five main species
In my home territory, the New Forest, the five main species are all present. One disillusioned acquaintance has had all of them in his

depleted garden at one time or another. Several people have two or three species visiting them, but one is usually predominant.

The colonisation of new areas by muntjac seems to have been the least noticed: it is much smaller and stealthier than other deer. One day there are none, and the next day they have settled in discreetly. The roe can also be shy and secretive, until it realises how easy it is to crop the roses growing in the Rectory garden. Bit by bit it asserts what it thinks are its rights, and becomes brazen in its indifference to the presence of humans. Only recently the managers of a nearby Golf Club found that their magnificent displays of tulips had been badly topped overnight. They suspected hooligans. But, some weeks later they realised that roe had taken up residence in the district, unseen and unreported, until a sharp-sighted gardener spotted some strange slot marks in a flower bed. The roe expert, Richard Prior, very aptly calls the roe the 'fairy of the woods', and many a countryman says of the roe that 'it can hide behind a blade of grass'. H. L. Edlin in *Forestry and Woodland Life* describes the roe as having a 'quaint elfin beauty'.

Antler formation

Some basic descriptions of the above may further help identification when a male is within view. A few other notes on individual characteristics have also been added.

RED DEER (*CERVUS ELAPHUS*)

This species will probably be the best known of all. It is our largest deer and is indeed Landseer's familiar 'Monarch of the Glen'. Its antlers are occasionally and ignobly downgraded to the role of a hatstand. A 'Royal' is a 12-pointer – three from the crown on top, and a brow, bay and tray tine – a magnificent sight and pretty unlikely to be seen in the average garden.

FALLOW DEER (*DAMA DAMA*)

This species is the traditional park deer, though others are sometimes similarly held in captivity. In early mediaeval times – and before – the deer parks were a source of winter food on the hoof. They are smaller than the Red deer, with a longer tail of about 12 in, which they are continually swishing about to keep off the flies, or just from habit. The antlers are not rounded or cylindrical like those of the red stags, but palmated or flattened. Not easy to confuse with other deer. The fallow

Red Deer *(Cervus elephus)*.

Fallow Deer *(Dama dama)*.

Photo: Norma Chapman

Muntjac *(Muntiacus reevesi) with velvet antlers (summer).*

Photo: Ken Macarthur

Roebuck Deer *(Capreolus capreolus)*

Photo: Mike Read

Sika *(Cervus nippon).*

Deer are sometimes nocturnal, or may arrive in an area
unnoticed. Signs of their presence include 'slot' marks, guard hair,
ivy browsed from tree trunks, droppings, scars or skid marks on
lawns, well-worn tracks, frayed shrubs, and damage to
plants above rabbit-reach.

The droppings (or fewmets) of deer are very different to those of rabbits.

Scars or skid marks in soft ground are quite common.

Slot of fallow.

Guard hair dropped in April.

Browsing height of fallow – with feet on the ground – shown by the ivy leaves stripped off in winter.

A regularly used track made by fallow.

- close to the house in broad daylight!
In recent years the habits of deer in many areas have changed.
They have become less afraid of humans, bolder and more intrusive.

Our 'resident' deer watching us watching them from their lodge, thirty-five yards from the author's kitchen.

Apple-bobbing, seen from an upstairs window, is a game that seems to intrigue the deer greatly.

Over thirty fallow in the field next to our house. Their 'targets' show up vividly.

Right: A young fallow trying to stare-out the author.

Below: Both deer are munching apples – viewed from a window fifteen yards away.

A fallow pricket, close to the house in broad daylight.

This young fallow, viewed from the bathroom, is alert but not unduly scared. The Belladonna lilies are rarely eaten, unlike some other lily species.

A fallow deer happily eating windfalls.

occasionally sport different coloured coats. As well as the normal bright chestnut (with white spots in summer) there are also creamy-white animals, and melanistic or black. Finally, there is the menil variety, which has a paler background colour than has the common fallow, with brighter spots.

SIKA DEER (*CERVUS NIPPON*).

Sometimes called the 'spotted deer'. A little smaller than the fallow: antlers are rounded – typically with four tines on each. Bright brown pelage (or coat).

ROE DEER (*CAPREOLUS CAPREOLUS*)

Smaller than the sika – only up to 29 in (74 cm) at the shoulder. Relatively large ears and thick neck. Antlers normally have three tines on each side: more like decorative little 'horns' or prongs that the branched attire of the larger stags. Foxy-red summer coat.

MUNTJAC, OR MORE COMMONLY REEVES' MUNTJAC (*MUNTIACUS REEVESII*): ALSO CALLED THE BARKING DEER

As already suggested, at first sight some observers would not think it was a deer at all. Bright brown, low to the ground and medium dog-sized. Short in-curved antlers on long furry pedicles, not much more than a single spike or horn. The bucks have small 'tusks' formed from the upper canines and used for fighting. Dogs have been attacked by muntjac defending their young.

The calls of deer

The 'voice', such as it is, varies according to the species. There are different bleats and barks issued for specific reasons, calling the young or demonstrating sudden fear, and from the red stags at rutting time there comes an unearthly, stomach-rumbling roaring and grunting, which can be very dramatic when heard echoing across a valley in the half-light. It is something of a ritual for continental hunters to go out at dawn and dusk and pay homage to the unseen warrior giving vent to his battle cry. For many a German – such is the reverence accorded- it might be a Wagner excerpt.

The sika also has a very distinctive call – a sort of screaming whistle followed by a belch, repeated at short intervals. It is unlike the voice of any other deer.

On the whole, deer are rather silent creatures, except during the rut. The staccato barks and the bleats are about the only other sounds in their repertoire.

Other differences

Some species (fallow and sika) have spots at certain times of the year, and others have none. Four out of the five species have short tails: the roe's appendage is virtually invisible. These points may assist with the identification of the females. Examining tracks or slots, or piles of droppings (fewmets) is a job for the expert: and damage at browsing height can be unreliable as some deer will stand on their back legs to reach what they want.

Some deer behave like herd animals and are gregarious in varying degrees. For much of the year the males stay together: the females with their young form a separate group. Others stay mostly in compact families. The muntjac is often solitary when not in its family group. Some, like roe, often have twins: fallow rarely; red deer *very* rarely and sika and muntjac never.

In the true wild state their diets and their habitats differ according to species, but deer are very adaptable creatures. The red deer of central Europe are really creatures of the forest edge, but in Scotland and our northern counties they have become acclimatised to living on open moorland with little else but scrub cover.

As to diet, the larger deer – red, fallow and sika – are mainly grazers, and the smaller deer – roe and muntjac – are mainly browsers, but there is a broad overlap in their food requirements. These vary from area to area, and according to what is available. Some, like the sika, will regularly eat quite large quantities of oddities like pine needles. Others are more conservative, though individuals will always do the unexpected. The way they eat also varies: some will feed steadily on whatever is around them, but the roe, although it has favourites upon which it will gorge until replete, is usually more 'picky'. It will take a little bit of this and a little bit of that, as it moves along a hedge or takes in samples of your garden. In my personal opinion, roe provide the best venison – perhaps because of their varied diet? I doubt that a lot of heather or coarse grasses would make the meat so flavoursome. Fallow also has a good flavour and texture, provided a young animal is chosen. A quotation from C. E. Hare's *The Language of Field Sports* says 'Buck-Venison is incomparable Food'. Never accept venison from an animal shot during the rut – even as a gift – or you will be put off deer-meat for ever! I believe it finds a market in German sausages.

Sensory faculties

The reactions of deer to humans is not always what is expected, as anyone who has them on their property will know. Their senses – sight, smell and hearing – are different to ours: the last two are much more acutely developed, as they are in dogs and other animals.

We do not yet know all there is about their vision, except that owing to the location of their eyes in the head and the design of the retina, I think I am right in saying that deer can see objects behind them. There are suggestions that at certain distances some deer do not see things in pin-sharp focus. If you stand stock-still in front of a deer, it may well stare back at you as though you were just an odd fencepost. But when you move, so will the deer – at speed. With the fallow in my garden, I sometimes play the children's staring game – standing like a statue – to see how long they will brazen it out. It entertains the weekend guests, watching from an upstairs window.

An amusing incident about the senses of roe deer was reported by a correspondent living near Winchester: 'Some weeks ago I surprised a doe which must have been asleep. She jumped up as I entered some bamboos and then stood with her back towards me. For five minutes she stood thus, twitching her ears at every sound. At length she turned and walked right up to me, before realising I was a human, and then she was away! I had been watching her from a distance of seven feet: it was a great experience'.

Was it sight or scent that triggered off her alarm system – or a bit of both?

Deer, roe in particular, can be very inquisitive and will linger near and even approach anything that arouses their curiosity. They will, for example, watch people at work from a comparatively short distance away: hurdle makers, men reparing forest gates and for all I know a man changing the wheel of a car.

Danger signals

For thousands of years deer have relied primarily on their sense of smell to warn them of danger. One whiff of an enemy upwind is enough to put them to flight long before they can actually see anything that might suggest a threat. The power of scenting varies with the species. A German biologist states that a red deer can wind

35

a human at over 1,200 m, while a fallow is restricted to only 200 m. Not everyone agrees that scenting is their main defence. In his classic 1951 book *The Roe Deer*, Henry Tegner asserts that the hearing of this woodland species is more developed that its sense of smell, 'as one would expect from an animal endowed with such long ears for its size'.

Certainly, when out stalking, absolute quiet is essential and not just the cracking underfoot of the proverbial dry twig, as mentioned on page one of every book on the subject. Making almost any sound that is not natural to the forest can cause immediate alarm. If, for example, a pair of binoculars hung around one's neck knock against the rifle – producing just a tiny metallic tap – a deer is likely to become instantly alert, and may take flight. The ears of deer are never still: always turning this way and that – even when lying down with eyes half-closed.

Deer walking round a garden, of course, behave differently, as already mentioned, having learned to accept certain household sounds as harmless. But those that are new and strange are likely to cause an instant reaction. I continue to be surprised by the way our local fallow pronk away after hearing just the tiny click of my camera shutter through an open window. Perhaps there is a future for the picturesque Japanese deer-scarer, operated by water trickling down a bamboo gutter and making a little 'click' as the bits of the wooden see-saw come together?

Colour vision

Not a lot seems to be known about a deer's colour vision. At one time it was thought that they only saw in various shades of grey or sepia or whatever it might be: something other than colour as we know it. However, recent research suggests that deer do have some perception of colour.

Many correspondents have written in to say that deer appear to have colour preferences when selecting things to eat or to avoid. I have always felt that *silver grey* foliage is one that they are wary of, but it may be that those plants (such as S*enecio maritima, Stachys byzantina* and a host of others) all have woolly or hairy leaves which the deer dislike, and that the colour has nothing to do with it. Other grey-leaved plants like lavender and sage, would have a strong taste: so we are now in the realms of co-incidence.

As for their preference for *blue* cranesbills (Johnson's Blue) as compared with the pink ones like Wargrave, the blue are nearly always eaten first. Perhaps the blue blossoms have more nectar in them, or the leaves are just tastier than the pink ones? Regarding crocuses, as mentioned earlier, it is nearly always the *yellow* ones that get taken first, particularly by sparrows. But wild primroses and daffodils are never eaten – nor are a host of other yellow plants – so the colour cannot be significant, just co-incidental.

The basic RHS list of plants which are 'relatively resistant' to deer, suggests that *purple-leaved* varieties of plants are possibly more attractive to deer than their green counterparts. No examples are given. In my recent survey, *Cotinus coggygria* (Nottcutts variety) which is purple, was reported as avoided by six gardeners, and as 'stripped' – or words to that effect – by seven others! A purple leaved hebe gets an all-clear, also a Euphorbia (but all euphorbias are avoided); and *Heuchera* (Palace Purple) remain untouched in different gardens: some of the purple-leaved acers were also resistant: as was the *'Atropurpurea' Ajuga* – and many other purple plants.

I doubt, therefore, if purple leaves are of much consequence. So the deer's selective process remains true to form – imponderable.

Chapter Four

Signs of Deer Visiting Gardens

Suspicions aroused

Some correspondents say that they never actually see their visiting deer. These are the nocturnal feeders or the dawn raiders – as yet shy of human activities. Visits to gardens by deer can start in a rather insidious way and take the householder by surprise, especially if he or she has not heard of any deer being in the district. The suspicion that something is amiss usually begins when a few areas of unusual plant damage, clearly not caused by rabbits, are suddenly noticed. Perhaps a couple of tubs of winter pansies cropped to the ground or some waist-high shoots of roses bitten off? This would be well-known deer villainy, but other early samplings might be much more subtle.

However, there are a number of signs that will identify the culprit beyond doubt:

The bite mark of a deer

The bite-mark of a deer when eating a stem the thickness of, say, a phlox or a camellia is not like a secateur-cut. The animal has no upper incisor teeth and cannot give a clean bite, so it pulls at the stem as its lower teeth engage with the hard pad of gum at the top, and this nearly always leaves a characteristic ragged 'tag' at the end. (See photo). This can be useful when deciding if some low-growing plants are being eaten by deer or rabbits, as the latter do not leave tags – their bite is clean cut. Sometimes bitten shoots are left on the ground.

Slot marks and droppings

Sooner or later deer tracks or slots which are not unlike those of sheep or goats, will be seen, as well as deer droppings – which are just a little different to those of rabbits. Sometimes they are scattered and sometimes in a plug, and at times they have a little pointed tip on one end. Size and shape vary according to the species of deer. Rabbit droppings, in contrast, are rounder and contain more fibrous matter.

Deer tracks

As the visits become more regular, well-worn tracks are likely to develop, leading from one or two favoured entry points. If any cover is in the way, it may be battered down. In my garden the deer have also created a slide down a steep bank, regularly used as a short-cut to one of their special patrol areas. Nothing grows here.

Trampling

Although deer are often described as agile and graceful, they can also be quite clumsy. When raiding our terrace at night in the search for anything new and edible, they often knock over quite large flower pots. They seem unable to step delicately between them! On one occasion a doe pushed over the top of a heavy stone 'mushroom', while rubbing her head against an old forsythia which was growing beside it.

Numerous reports have been received about the trampling of plants, particularly if they are growing across any regular access route. In my case it is a young lavender hedge that has suffered over the last three years. The lavender is very brittle, and when the deer stand on it – which they do frequently – stems are often broken away from the main plant. I am continually buying replacements. Letters have described many varieties of plants being 'battered out of existence'. There was a particularly sad story of a bed of roses which had been underplanted with statice (sea lavender). This had been flattened while the deer had stood there cropping the roses. A double insult! To explain that such vandalism is incidental or accidental does nothing to soothe an infuriated husbandman.

Lawns

On lawns, ruts and furrows up to 3 ft in length will sometimes be seen, as well as little pits which could be confused with those made by grey squirrels. Holes made by badgers excavating for earth-worms tend to be more determined and less haphazard. I'm never quite sure why the larger deer – such as the local fallow – make holes in lawns, though they are known to dig down for edible material in suitable places. We have truffles in the New Forest, but as far as I know, not in my garden!

In wet weather deer will sometimes make skid marks, which can be quite deep. Most people will know that deer often paw the ground like horses, and this can add to the minor scarring of the turf. It can be a part of the territory-marking process, though not usually on lawns. And when the young are playing and head-butting they will inevitably make some scuff-marks, but this must be of little consequence compared to the fun of seeing the kids or fawns at play. If I had a velvety croquet lawn I might feel different. The gardeners who reported the various items of damage to their lawns did so with some irritation! Moles were bad enough to contend with, but deer as well . . .

Resting area

According to how possessive the local deer become about their gardens, so they may decide to make a resting or sleeping place – the lodge or lair – usually formed from a 'nest' of dead leaves, as far as fallow are concerned. This will only occur if the garden is large enough and has sufficient cover.

Guard hair

Another piece of evidence of deer visits will be the tufts of guard or cast hair found at moulting time. Each tuft is quite substantial, and much used for nest-lining by our long tailed tits.

Damage to tree bark

Badly scarred trees, saplings or tall shrubs can be very unsightly. Deer will strip or rub off bark for different reasons. Fraying by roe, if seen in a local woodland, is often the first sign that they have moved into the area. There are two categories of damage: *bark strip-ping* when the bark is peeled away and then eaten, and *fraying* when the bark is scraped off the tree by the antlers as part of the 'anointing' process. In this, the male deer deposits his individual scent from glands on the forehead to stake out his territory against a rival.

The different deer species have somewhat different preferences

40

for the trees they attack. Choice is governed by height, girth, age, smooth or rough bark and so on. Local 'forest' fallow seem to prefer broad-leaved species like beech, chestnut and willow, though they will also tear away the resiny bark of young Douglas firs and go for Christmas trees (Norway spruce). Luckily for gardeners, the more numerous roe seem less keen on stripping and eating bark, except in severe weather. The damage they do is mostly fraying.

In woodlands, if there is a solitary tree of a different species – say, a lone pine in an oak plantation or vice versa – deer will often choose this stray specimen for fraying. (So a Head Forester informs me concerning the red deer in Portugal).

Fraying is also done to remove the 'velvet' (the furry skin covering the growing antlers) when it has completed its protective role. When clean of velvet, this rubbing may continue and locally is called 'burnishing'. Fraying will show no toothmarks, only the scoring of antlers. A local ranger tells me that every year he watches juvenile fallow bucks with their first set of antlers rubbing their heads in among the thistle tops. This they do as the velvet dries, when the little horns are probably tender and itchy. When older they progress to suitable shrubs and saplings, which are springy and flexible.

In my garden they have almost demolished an old broom. Several stems were rubbed bare by a buck, aided by a doe, and some of the plant was broken down completely. On another occasion (one January) while watching from a window, I saw about five fallow (buck, does and a pricket) investigating a mature forsythia. All of them seemed to take turns at gnawing the bark, leaving discernible toothmarks. In due course, after pushing and rubbing their foreheads, they snapped off three of the brittle stems. One doe was also involved in the head-thrusting – odd for a female with no scent glands and no antlers! The pricket took part in the gnawing; a local deer-consultant suggested that young animals will do this to help dislodge their milk-teeth.

Muntjac have also been reported as 'tearing at young saplings – stripping off the bark and then abandoning the remains . . .' I suspect this would have been caused by fraying with antlers and tusks. The same writer had to wire in all his young apple trees to save them from being demolished. Another had to protect his plum trees.

As to eating bark, at some stage the normal appetite for leaves, shoots, buds, flowers and 'greenstuff' can develop into bark-stripping. Deer need fibre in their diet, and this is certainly one reason why they scar the trees in this way. Red, sika and fallow are the main culprits – the damage usually being done in the winter.

Fraying posts

Deer will often adopt an unfortunate young tree or bush as their chosen 'fraying post', just as a cat will have its favourite area for sharpening claws – often the best velvet curtains. If you tidy up a deer's fraying place, it will almost certainly choose another of your most desirable shrubs. This being so, it is probably more sensible to leave it until it is completely demolished, though it does become tedious explaining to everyone who asks why it is there.

Thrashing

This performance consists of a male deer flaying branches, small trees, or low cover such as brambles, heather and so on, with its antlers. In my garden the fallow stand under some very tall laurels and shake their antlers in the branches overhead, with such ferocity that they manage to break off branches and bring down showers of leaves. I have also seen deer thrashing overhead cover on the sides of woodland rides on many occasions. I do not know why they do it. I think perhaps to let off steam when they are stressed. A forest keeper told me that he felt it was loosely connected with territory claiming – perhaps an immature buck feeling his way? In gardens, very little harm comes of it.

Girdling

I have described bark-stripping and fraying, though more of a problem in large woodlands than private gardens, because the scars on the trees really do stand out and ornamental trees in gardens quite often suffer. One friend has replaced some shrub he was given as a present three times, in order not to offend the donor! Somehow he couldn't get around to enclosing it in a protective cage, or perhaps he hated the sight of netting.

Serious bark-stripping involving all-round girdling can result in the death of quite large and valuable trees as a result of dessication, decay, fungal infection and so on. However, wounds which do not circle a tree usually grow a protective callous over the exposed surface and survive. Grey squirrels will also pull off the outer bark of trees – beech and sycamore being the most vulnerable.

A possible antidote

To alleviate the problem of bark damage, the managers of a Dorset arboretum (mostly hardwoods) are leaving horizontal piles of tree prunings on the ground, in the hope that the deer (roe and fallow) will go for them in preference to their valuable trees. The prunings – carried out from January onwards – are up to 6 ft in length. The trials have been underway for two seasons, so more time is needed before positive recommendations can be made, but interim results seem promising. The idea has the merit of simplicity and minimal cost.

Bark damage and how to limit it has been very carefully studied by the forestry authorities and there is a great deal of literature on the subject.

Other signs of deer in the area

These include play rings, wallows, cast antlers and so on – though not usually in gardens. All are easily recognisable.

CHAPTER FIVE

BEHAVIOUR IN GARDENS

This is not a general treatise on deer, but a few observations on their behaviour in gardens may help to understand them better – and go some way towards limiting damage. I have already said that the feeding habits of deer are unpredictable. Their likes and dislikes vary from year to year and garden to garden, so it would be quite reasonable for me to dodge this issue altogether. However, for those who may only recently have been exposed to the presence of deer peering in through their windows, I will include a few scattered thoughts on the subject.

We are now accustomed to the fact that deer in increasing numbers are content to leave their traditional habitats and take up residence in the vicinity of houses – with human smells and noises, motor cars, dogs and so on. There are a number of reasons why they should do this.

Particular attraction of gardens

As the deer population expands and the competition for territories becomes more intense, unsuccessful males and sub-dominant females – sometimes with their young – will be on the move and are the most likely ones to come into our gardens. Once they discover a source of food that they like, they remember the location and return again and again, until eventually they adopt you. There may also be other added attractions – apart from the food – such as escape cover, shade, fraying material, a comfortable lodge that they have taken over and so on. At this stage they are difficult to get rid of: you have become an official territory.

My experience with fallow and roe is that these uninvited females (and their young) cause most of the damage in gardens. Bucks come and go. Theoretically, if you remove the occupant, you create a vacuum which in due course will be filled up by the next animal in the queue. Thankfully, as regards gardens, this does not always happen.

Gardens are on the whole a particularly attractive form of habitat: they provide much more variety of food in a concentrated area, than most woodlands, or modern farms where monoculture and large fields are prevalent, or open moorland. Such an extended choice of diet is appreciated.

Inclination to sample

While deer are fairly conservative in their main dietary choices, they are also quite keen to have a nibble here and a nibble there, in case they should chance on something delectable that they have not met with before. They are adventurous: they will never have seen, say, delphiniums or runner beans in a wood, but they will happily try them out in a garden. When deer are 'moved' from one location to another, it is noticeable that during the first few days, they will often go over the ground carefully and undertake a lot of sampling. There will be some plants that are be new to them and are eaten simply because they taste good, and others that perhaps fulfil a nutritional need.

Essential nutrients

Deer will instinctively feed on material that contains nutrients that are essential to their welfare. Obviously, when they are getting over a lean winter, or when the males are building up their strength before and after the breeding season, or growing antlers or in the case of the females, when preparing for lactation, or recovering from stress, they will seek out vital 'tonic' foods. Some of these may be more available in gardens than on, say, open scrublands or in a soft-wood plantation. Garden plants that are treated with fertilisers are known to be more attractive to deer, and gardens that are well-watered – and therefore greener than the surrounding land – will provide slightly earlier crops. A garden with a variety of flowers, vegetables, shrubs, weeds and grasses can be both a health food shop for deer, as well as a delicatessen.

Regarding their special nutritional needs, a German colleague, who had studied deer all his life, one day observed that the red deer hinds were eating large quantities of nettle tops, while the stags were ignoring them. Thinking that this would be of riveting interest to a local Saxon farmer, who was driving past in an old bullock cart, he told him of his observations. The old peasant didn't even bother to look round, but said: 'My family have been feeding nettles to our house cows for hundreds of years . . .' Field observations later showed that the flowers of the Giant Nettle (*Urtica dioica*) were being selected during the animals' high lactation period. Further, when various seeds were sifted out from the red deer faeces and germinated, the results showed that a high proportion of nettles were being eaten from June to August, confirming the link with a milk-stimulating diet.

None of this need for nutrients at certain times of the year explains why so many people wrote in and said, for example: 'For the first time in five years, the deer have suddenly started to eat my sedums', or whatever it might have been. We just have to accept the illogicality in their choice of diet. Individual deer have individual tastes, so it may be that you have a sedum-eating deer visiting you, or a particularly keen sampler.

I am aware that none of this is very scientific. We know exactly what dietary constituents are required to grow healthy antlers, for example, but we do not know if there is any dietary reason why they eat the blooms of tulips, but not daffodils. Are the tulip petals just more palatable, or do they contain some important nutrients required at this time of year? They also eat the 'leaves' of bluebells, but not the flowers, and the flowers of pelargoniums, but rarely the leaves. Taste and texture must surely have something to do with it, and, possibly – toxicity.

Toxic plants

A friend, who knows a lot about the game animals of Austria, told me that the deer never ate the lilies of the valley or the hellebores growing wild in the mountains because they are poisonous. Others taking part in the survey often made the same comment about poisonous plants in general, but never provided any factual evidence.

I was unconvinced. However, studying the excellent wall chart of the poisonous plants prepared by *Gardening WHICH*, I now see that of the two dozen toxic garden plants, nearly all are avoided by deer. (The list is basic: not fully comprehensive). Ivy is an exception, and yew is in a different category in that it is safe when green, but toxic when withered and half dried up. As well as lilies of the valley and hellebores already mentioned, among the toxic plants are autumn

46

crocus, Daphne mezereum, euphorbia, laburnum, lantana, oleander, datura and others – none normally eaten by deer. (Others listed on the wall chart are classed as irritants etc. but not really poisonous). Although it is something of a generalisation I think there may be something in this toxicity element which may help us in our selection of deer-resistant plants. But to confuse the issue, ruminants – with their two or three stomach compartments – are able to cope with some toxins, unlike other animals with only one.

Influence of colours

I am hesitant to raise the question of colour preference again – having already discussed it in connection with yellow crocuses. This example was confused because sparrows as well as deer were also showing a preference for yellow. But the phenomenon will not go away. Recently, a correspondent reported that her fallow deer 'ate all the yellow lupins out of a bed of *mixed* colours'. One wonders why?

What constitutes palatability or the reverse?

I can find no common denominator as to why deer avoid certain plants, other than the toxicity already mentioned. Their idea of what is palatable or unpalatable might be difficult to define.

They will eat plants that have thorns and spikes, like brambles, roses, holly and hawthorn, but as suggested earlier, I suspect that some 'textures' such as hairy, downy leaves may be unattractive to them. (Lambs Ears, for example). They seem to avoid some plants with strong-smelling leaves or flowers, like lavender, rosemary, sage and so on. Choisya leaves, when torn, smell strongly of tom-cat. Catmint itself is pretty powerful, as is ordinary mint, and all are avoided. Santolina is another on the 'safe' list, which has a peculiar 'herby' smell, which some people apparently find quite refreshing, but I think it might be unpleasant on the tongue.

But we are not on safe ground, with our ideas of strong smells. Deer will chew resiny bark and will sometimes eat the leaves of young eucalyptus, though not regularly or in quantity.

I am not puzzled by their avoiding vegetation which seems to have a very pungent or positive taste, but why should they avoid plants which are apparently bland or neutral, like peonies, which they never touch? My herb book tells me that 'all parts of this plant – especially the flowers – are poisonous', so perhaps this is the reason? Rabbits also avoid peonies.

The *Gardening WHICH* list could be considerably extended, I think. This passing thought was prompted by wondering why rhubarb *leaves* are never eaten – they are toxic, to humans. It may be difficult to differentiate between what deer can tolerate, compared to humans, but I feel sure there is a link. Of course, there are some puzzling exceptions. Berberry – sometimes eaten by deer – is classed as poisonous (apart from the berries) in my herb book.

Peak periods of damage

Deer are active both by day and by night, but the time when they probably do the most damage is at first light. All is quiet and they are unlikely to be disturbed. As to seasonal damage, with few exceptions, most people agreed that there were peak periods of the year when deer visited gardens and caused the most harm. This was from the late winter until the spring. Obviously, they are at their hungriest during the winter months. In many gardens the worst destruction was in the early spring, not the sharp grey days of January and February, though in my case this is when the fallow start feeding on my camellia leaves as a priority, and then anything else that happens to be in their path. Typical comments included: 'They go somewhere else during the summer months'. . . 'Even our "tame" roe; takes a summer break'. . .; 'During the summer very little is taken, other than the roses'. Of course, they will also take advantage of anything else that tempts them at the same time – particularly tender green growth in the vegetable garden, ripe strawberries, and such obvious delicacies.

The start of the deer's summer holiday usually coincides with the females going into deeper cover, where they can find more privacy to give birth to their young. The approximate breeding periods are: red deer – early June onwards; fallow – mid-May through June; sika – much the same; and roe – the main ravager of gardens – end-April peaking in May. The muntjac is different: it is a non-seasonal breeder and does can be seen with fawns during any period of the year. By the time the females have been away from our gardens for two or three weeks, we are approaching high summer and food is plentiful almost everywhere. In our case, over two consecutive seasons our lodger brought her fawn back to show us in mid-June when it was only about three or four days old – and stayed on! But as already explained, our garden is something of an oasis in the rather bare Forest surroundings.

The males also seem to take a summer break, because they equally have less need for garden produce at this time, and possibly because the average garden does not afford suitable conditions for activities concerned with pairing and territory forming. But there will always be a few lone wandering bucks.

One dissenting voice from Sussex complained that, 'The roe were particularly active during the summer months,' without offering any reason, which was probably wise of him. And from Oban, 'Some summers there is no break at all,' but this is not that common.

The weather effect

In the summer of 1995 the drought in our area was particularly severe and the ground very parched. This caused a number of plants on the hitherto UNEATEN list to be transferred to the EATEN list. For instance, the deer ate down all the mature courgette plants – with their tough fibrous stalks and hairy leaves. They naturally ate the 'fruits'. A bed of nasturtiums was completely cropped for the first time, as well as other hitherto unattractive plants. Presumably they all had a high moisture content.

Deer do not drink regularly like horses or cattle, though from time to time we see them sipping from pools and streams. It has been suggested that if one provided a source of water in very dry weather, it might protect our thirst-quenching plants, like the fleshy Sedum 'Ice-plant'. Personally, I think that it is more likely to provide them with an added incentive for a visit, like a salt-lick, which is sometimes advocated. During the drought, we never saw the deer drinking from our pool, though they were very often close to it. Other gardeners observed their pools being used from time to time.

Diets of different deer species

The different species have slightly different food choices, which one would expect between the browsers and the grazers. But there is a very broad overlap. If any really odd item is reported as being devoured in a garden, I can assume a muntjac is responsible. Two or three correspondents have written about their tame muntjac. One, allegedly very spoiled, enjoys kiwi fruit, and another gets into the owner's greenhouse and steals his cucumbers and tomatoes. But domesticated deer of any species would be capable of almost anything.

Chapter Six

Deterrents

Patchy results from survey

A great number of people responded to the questions on deterrents. The majority were reported as 'absolutely useless', but there were a number of partial successes. A few seemed convinced that they had, at any rate for a while, succeeded in protecting vital areas of their gardens and lessened attacks in general – *in their own particular set of circumstances.* In such cases one has to ask if the cessation of damage to plants was coincidental with other factors. For instance, had the deer just moved out of the area for the time being? Had culling taken place nearby; had any holding cover in the area just been cut down, or was it a time of the year when certain plants had lost their seasonal appeal, and so on? With many plants there is a definite season of maximum palatability, as we humans appreciate with asparagus, new potatoes, rhubarb and so on.

Conditions in different gardens also vary so much that they can have an effect on the potency or otherwise of any deterrent. As well as the edibility, the variety and the rarity value of what is on offer can determine whether the deer stay or go, regardless of the deterrent. If a garden has been rendered somewhat hostile to the deer, are there alternative pleasure grounds for them just down the road? It will make a difference.

For reasons that are not always clear, it is apparent that *what fails in one garden may very well work in another.* I believe some deer groups react quite differently to others. They have varied likes and dislikes. This being so, I would advise anyone to try a suitable deterrent – expecting the worst. Most are inexpensive: some cost nothing at all. And to give them a fair chance, obey the instructions or follow any advice that is available. Where chemical sprays and other short term devices are in use, remember to renew the application after the stated period, or heavy rain, baking hot sun and so forth. Correspondents confessed that they did not always do this. Proprietary sprays tend to be expensive. It is appreciated that deer get used to almost anything in time – so it is advisable to keep two or three different deterrents on the go. If it is something in the scarecrow category, keep changing its position at regular intervals.

Trouble can be expected with almost any *new plantings*. Deer are very curious and will sample – and even pull up – particularly colourful plants over a period of a few days until they get bored. Just keep replanting them! My advice would be to use a deterrent, or give some form of protection in the early days. Protective netting for new shrubs is dealt with in chapter nine. A professional horticulturist wrote: 'I have regularly seen newly planted shrubs stripped when first put in the ground. As the plant matures, or the novelty wears off, they are totally ignored. I have had the same experience many times.'

A lady also described how she planted a group of heathers (*Erica cinerea*) which were immediately torn out and left scattered around the lawn. She replanted them, netted them, and they survived. I had the same experience with hybrid primroses – pulled up the day after planting, hardly nibbled at all, and put back in the patio containers without loss. Rabbits will also disinter small plants.

Anti-fox deterrents
This is not quite the red herring it may seem. I have included it to show that some animals can be successfully scared away from their 'target' when confronted with the right deterrent, probably for a certain length of time only. The protection of partridge nests from foxes and other predators that hunt by scent has worked pretty well for over a hundred years, and is illustrated as an example.

I spent the whole of my professional working life with the Game Conservancy, which naturally involved collaborating with gamekeepers. At one time we had an experimental estate of 4,000 acres, where we studied the management of wild partridges and other game. One of the keepers' routine tasks every spring was to find as many of the partridge nests as possible, and monitor their progress very discreetly during the twenty-four-day incubation period. Up to 200 nests would be under observation every season. Of the nests that were destroyed during the sitting period, about half were lost as a result of agricultural operations (silage cutting etc.), and half due to attacks by foxes, corvids, rats, stoats, weasels, feral cats and so on.

To protect the nests from predators that hunted by scent, the keepers used to dress the nests with a few drops of one or other of the proprietary products like Renardine, or some secret formula of their own, no doubt handed down by a grandfather: or just 'spend a penny' near the nest, leaving a human scent on the ground. All were pretty effective – the latter as good as any. Many of the proprietary chemicals sold for the purpose contained a tarry-smelling substance in a base of some sort of animal oil. It is known that foxes – and rabbits – avoid such smells.

For the first and last three days of the sitting period, the hen partridge is at her most vulnerable. At the start she is inclined to be a bit fidgety, not yet sitting really tight down, and some of her body scent escapes from under her. At the end, when the eggs are starting to chip, she will raise herself up a little, and the scent is no longer sealed in. This is when most of the kills occur. By masking her give-away smell, keepers are able to protect scores of nests that would otherwise be predated. I will deal with the effects of Renardine – and urine – on deer on page 00.

If, by chance, a bird is attacked, but escapes – probably deserting her nest for a few days – a keeper will put the abandoned eggs in an incubator and substitute artificial ones in the nest, thus avoiding the real eggs getting chilled and the embryos dying. At the chipping stage the keeper will return the salvaged eggs to the nest and the hen partridge will hatch out her brood, oblivious of the drama that has taken place.

Evicting deer from silage crops – a potential death trap

Risking another red herring, I think it may be worth reporting the success of lion dung when used as a deterrent – in this case synthesised as a concentrated liquid.

Some years ago an increasing number of farmers began to voice their concern over the killing and maiming of roe deer kids that were either born in silage crops, or put down to rest there while their mothers went off to feed. The casualties occurred when the grass-cutters harvested the crop, though sometimes nothing was apparent until a bale was broken open some months later and the mummified remains of a kid found inside. To prevent such accidents, all that was needed was a 'chemical fence' around the crop for a day or two before it was cut. One of the big chemical companies took up the challenge as a side issue: it was actually working on long-term protection needs, such as young forestry plantations and so on. I believe it also undertook trials to keep antelopes out of mango groves.

I was one of the inspecting team which visited the silage crop trial areas over three seasons. So far as we could judge, not a single casualty occurred in any of the treated fields. Other deterrents such as the flashing lamps used by road repair engineers were also effective at scaring deer out of the crops for a short period. Confirming this success, a lady from near Uckfield wrote, 'Having lost all the September roses, we had a good display in the middle of November – having put out a flashing traffic light'.

In the early days of the trials – using fallow deer in parks – a video was made showing the deer approaching their usual feed containers, unaware that they had been 'doctored' with the lion dung concentrate. When the animals were about twenty yards away from the feed, they suddenly stopped in their tracks, leaped high in the air, and ran off terrified! Interesting, when one thinks that they had never seen a lion. It must have been an inherited instinct that had been dormant for thousands of years.

The synthetic lion dung is currently undergoing Ministry safety checks for possible toxicity, but it would probably be too costly, and unsuitable in other ways, for regular use in gardens. Fresh lion dung is dealt with on page 56.

The law and garden deterrents

Having mentioned the Ministry checks, I should state that there are some odd restrictions in place regarding some of the deterrents – chemical and otherwise – that are used in gardens. In answer to a question on this matter, the Pesticides Safety Directorate (York) stated 'the use of lion dung and human hair are covered by the scope of the Control of Pesticides Regulations (1986) and are *not* approved for use as pesticides . . .' It would seem that the PSD – however well meaning – are really operating in a world of fantasy, if they class gatherings of human hair, encased in old tights and strung about the rose bushes, as 'pesticides'. *Websters International Dictionary* says a 'pesticide is an agent used to *destroy* a pest,' – not to deter or frighten one away. With untested chemicals – home-made or otherwise – one would have to be circumspect, and it would be wise to seek advice regarding special permits.

An amusing comment came from a retired Army officer whose winter pansies had all been topped by roe. He wrote: 'Judging by my wife's comments, any deterrent would have to be terminal.' Many of us know the feeling !

Reports on Individual Repellent Substances

Dependent on smell

SCUTTLE
(Fine Agrochemicals Ltd, 3 The Bull Ring, Worcester, WR2 5AA)
Described as 'an approved repellent' and non-toxic. It is a derivative of natural fish oils and possesses a smell and taste which is repugnant to sensitive animals such as rabbits and deer. Effect usually apparent for 30–80 days. Can be sprayed or painted on. Only a few gardeners reported using this product. Comments included:

> 'Does not work on tender young leaf' – otherwise generally good when used undiluted.'
> 'Ineffective in protecting *Cornus*. Regarding *Hostas* – safeguarded them totally one year, but was comparatively ineffective the following . . . On the whole worth using – when sprayed on a few roses (mostly rugosas) they were untouched'.
> 'Seems to be effective for several weeks, but depends on rainfall . . .'

KORNITOL
(Made in Germany, but used in one garden in Hampshire against roe).
> 'Successful in blocking entry points'.

FOWICAL
Three reports saying 'very effective'. Claimed to be non-toxic and formulated for use against deer, hares and rabbits, but now no longer available in the UK because of current regulations, and high cost of registration. For German/Austrian readers it can still be purchased in those countries, where it is manufactured by Forst Chemie of Ettenheim. D7637.

AA PROTECT
Used successfully by the Forestry Commission for many years for protecting woodlands against deer, hares and rabbits. Unsuitable for gardens as it is essential to wear protective clothing, gloves, face mask etc.

STAY-OFF
Only suitable for cats and dogs.

HOPPIT
No longer manufactured, although still mentioned in some magazine articles.

HAIR – HUMAN AND OTHER.
Several letters started: 'I know this sounds silly but . . .' and then continue about human hair. 'A friend of a friend' had told them it was a good deer deterrent. In some districts this was obviously well-known, judging by the reaction of the local hairdressers who were evidently quite ready to oblige fraught customers. All the recipes said that the hair had to be *unwashed:* it was the human scent that was the secret, and Pink Carnation shampoo would spoil the effect. In some of the cases where it failed, I wonder if this had been the reason? That and – like all deterrents that depended on smell – the fact that it had not been renewed sufficiently often. 'It loses its potency after summer rain,' said one lady.

The hair is normally packed into an 'envelope' of old nylon tights or muslin bags and hung about the vulnerable bushes – usually roses – at the nose height of the deer. A few people found this array rather unattractive and put the hair into the orange netting bags used by supermarkets as containers for citrus fruits, sprouts and other such produce. Others disliked the whole procedure and gave up trying.

The deterrent effect of the hair is said to last longer if the nylon or netting container is protected by a light plastic bag, left open at the bottom.

Some of the 'failed' trials were pretty convincing: one lady (whose daughter was a hairdresser, by chance) used the hair against roe 'on several occasions on twenty-eight rose bushes – but to no avail'. On the other hand a professional nurseryman in Scotland used it successfully on individual vulnerable plants or in a small ring-fenced area enclosing particularly edible plants. He obtained small sackfuls of hair from his own barber, so probably much less washed than from a ladies' salon. 'It was,' he said ' a time-consuming operation,' as he often had 100–200 lots out at the same time, replaced monthly, between January and April, which was his most difficult season. If it hadn't been 'quite effective' to use his own words, I doubt if he would have taken all that trouble.

One of the more successful users hung the bags in the gaps where the deer entered the garden during periods of peak activity. But from a retired Colonel a convincing: 'I used to try to protect a few roses by hanging up bags of hair from the barbers shop at the Guards Depot. You would think this would deter anything – but not roe!' From New Jersey: 'Combings from my sizeable beard has worked well for twenty-eight years . . .'

The ratio of success to failure was about one-to-two, so at least there were *some* satisfied customers.

DOG HAIR

From Vancouver Island BC: 'Deer will stay out of any garden if you tie small bags of dog hair to the rose bushes, or above your tulips'. This was confirmed by another report from Manitoba. Perhaps dog hair has the edge on us humans, as wolves are natural predators of deer; and whereas hounds hunt deer instinctively, to some extent, they have to be trained to hunt the fox.

The results were inconclusive again, but I picked up a few tips – should I decide to try out the human hair offensive in my own garden.

LION DUNG

Zoos and safari parks are reported to have been very helpful with supplies. Warnings were given about the overpowering smell of ammonia given off by the dung. Seven users reported complete success, and only one dissented – having seen both fallow and muntjac walk right over it. (No details were given regarding condition – fresh or stale – of the dung).

One lady discontinued its use because her spaniel always rolled in it: another eventually gave it up – though successful – because it never broke down and mixed in with the soil. One year later it remained on the surface of her rose beds 'still looking just like lion dung'.

There were the usual comments about sun and rain exhausting

the scent, and the nuisance of having to get fresh supplies. One gardener who used it just for blocking various deer entrances said that they 'merely chose different points of entry', but this can happen with any deterrent. Only one person mentioned how long the potency lasted; it was still working well after six weeks of cold, hungry weather, when the deer would have been tempted to enter the garden for food. Unfortunately, the writer did not say how long after this the 'barrier effect' persisted. It was reported that 'a pet cat took a keen interest, but was not disturbed by the dung'. Another very considerate lady declined to try it because she thought her horses might have a fit.

MOTHBALLS

An expatriate from Sussex, now living in Brazil, recommended mothballs: 'No wild animal likes the smell, and none will pass . . . they should be put in small muslin or similar bags and strung up at deer's head height at intervals of about five feet (with one on the ground every three feet if also troubled by rabbits)'. He still uses them in Brazil, but against other animals.

The idea sounded attractive to me: reasonably cheap and a slow-release operation, with no messy liquids involved. So I did some trials in tubs full of mixed flowers near the house. First, I used a single mothball hidden in the centre of each tub. Almost immediately three out of five gazania blooms were eaten, a foot away from the mothball. I then placed two mothballs on the edge of each tub, but some more plants – mimulus and petunias – were partly eaten, and the mothballs knocked to the ground. I increased the dose to three mothballs and some desultory nibbling continued. In any case, the plants were 'second choices', but it was during a drought and the deer were much less fussy – just keen to get moisture.

The tubs were on our terrace, close to a bed of tobacco flowers, *regale* and oriental hybrid lilies, and jasmine. But when sitting out on a summer's evening, the smell of mothballs sometimes over-powered the sweet floral scents. As the drought got worse, the tobaccos were badly topped by the deer. To test the staying power of the mothballs I hung some out on a washing line: exposed to all weathers: they lasted over eight weeks.

A second successful report concerning fallow came in from East Sussex. In spite of their failure in my garden, I propose to repeat the trials, but modified here and there.

RENARDINE

This was probably the most commonly tried repellent – well-known for successfully keeping rabbits and foxes at bay. It was not, as far as I know, formulated to deal with deer, and my requests for basic information from the manufacturers went unanswered.

The failure rate which was reported very positively was twice as high as the success – or partial success – rate. The latter reports were sometimes a little vague and said that the product had *seemed* to work, from which I assumed some improvement in the condition of the plants under protection must have been noticed. Sometimes a comment was made that though it was to some extent helpful in the battle against raiding deer, it had to be renewed too often (approx 7 – 10 days), and after a while this became too expensive.

As with other deterrents it was sometimes used to protect specially valuable plants, as opposed to making a 'chemical fence' around a whole flower bed. In the latter case lengths of string or cord were soaked in the liquid. One lady used old tennis balls drenched in the chemical, mounted on bamboo sticks. More usually little ribbons of impregnated cloth were tied to the sticks. A friend of mine, who had been troubled by roe topping some lilies in his woodland garden, devised a very successful method of application. This involved soaking little blocks of sawn wood in the liquid. After scattering them around the lilies, the damage ceased and in this case never re-started.

CREOSOTE

This familiar wood-tar distillate was tried by a number of people, possibly because it was cheaper than any of the special products sold as animal repellents, and it is known that rabbits dislike it. As usual, the results were mixed (about equal), but in this case the evidence on the ground was more convincing than the numbers alone. The pro-creosote users invariably said that it *seemed* to work. Such cautious appraisals suggested that perhaps other factors might also have been at work. However, two positive results were reported: when a rag soaked in creosote was hung in the middle of a camellia bush, from which the buds had been regularly eaten by roe – and occasionally red deer – the damage stopped abruptly. In another garden regularly visited by roe which did enormous damage, creosoted rags were hung up at entry points and *the deer stopped their raids.* Plants like bluebells – normally cropped heavily – and many others started to grow again. The creosote was renewed every 6–8 weeks.

Clothes pegs are useful for hanging up rags, and a plastic spray canister makes subsequent applications quite quick. From the West Country a lady wrote that she had used non-plastic binder twine soaked in creosote and stretched along the fence tops, with success against the red deer. But she said they were still very wild and wary.

A lady from Inverness-shire reported (end of May) that her creosoted ropes placed 4 ft above the ground around her borders and vegetable plots had 'so far proved successful'. However, the following year, in June, she wrote that the ropes had *not* been infallible. Her ready-to-eat strawberries had been totally cropped, and in late August she had actually seen a young roe stepping between two of the horizontal ropes to attack some flowers.

The 'antis' were very positive, reporting it as 'completely useless'! Different results in different seasons were often reported, but should not necessarily be a reason for giving up. Finally, a local deer expert told me that he had seen a roe licking a wooden high-seat that he had treated with a wood preservative only the day before. What can one say? An eccentric individual? Jeyes Fluid had been used by one gardener with success against muntjac, but the treatment (dipped rags on sticks) was applied *every evening* to individual rose bushes.

BLOOD PRODUCTS

In addition to being mentioned by the nurseryman in California, (see under 'Home Made Deterrents'), another American lady recommended that dried blood or blood meal should be 'spread around the garden' to keep away the white-tailed deer. At home two other gardeners had heard about it, but could give no details other than that it had successfully prevented deer from using their normal entry routes to a property.

Somewhat related to this was a strange ritual that occurred in the New Forest more than 20 years ago.

An old lady, for whom I can vouch, was having trouble with a fallow buck that had invaded her rather isolated garden and was creating a great deal of damage. She saw no alternative but to ask a local forester to remove it. In due course he arrived with a friend, and shot the buck. He then suggested that she went indoors while they carried out some procedure that would ensure no other deer would enter her garden 'for a long time'. She thinks that they dragged the body of the freshly killed animal around the boundary, but doesn't really know. And, improbable as it sounds, no deer came into her garden for five years! One cannot, of course, read too much into this, because in those days, the deer population was much smaller and they rarely left their haunts to raid gardens. But, having lived in the Forest for nearly fifty years, I like to believe those two commoners knew what they were doing.

SCENTED SOAP

A deer consultant, who works in the district, reported that to protect an avenue of young limes that were being regularly damaged by red deer thrashing, tablets of strongly scented soap had been hung up in the trees at nose height. No damage had occurred during the three years since the consultant was last in touch. Another gardener, troubled by both fallow and muntjac, also succeeded in keeping the deer out of her garden by hanging bits of soap in the trees around her house. This was originally done to protect her two cherry trees, from which both leaves and fruit were regularly eaten. No further damage occurred, and she since reported a deer-free year and lots of flowers, though she did wonder if it was just a coincidence. A third just said that 'it had worked'.

My own trials on camellia bushes which are always shredded by the fallow sometime after Christmas, consisted of hanging up small squares of Wright's Coal Tar soap in four bushes in early December. After three months of winter rain, at least the soap had hardly diminished in size – though one sample showed mouse tooth marks – and I think the smell was still unaffected, though never very strong. The slow release of the tarry odour was also a good feature. After seven weeks, three of the bushes that had been badly attacked in previous years, were once again shredded up to within 12 in to 18 in of the piece of soap. The leaves were small and tender, as they were the regrowth following the attack of the previous year. Elsewhere, a mature bush lasted slightly longer before nibbling started, and the damage was less severe, or rather more desultory.

On 1 February I put out some cubes of lavender soap on two other smaller bushes which had not then been attacked. In time some nibbling did take place, but it was less intense.

I suspect that the cubes of soap were too small to be effective, or that I should have used more on each bush. Lavender had the edge over the coal-tar. The coloured pendants looked quite decorative in the bleak January weather! At last we may have a use for all those horrible little bits of soap that are given away free – along with the shower caps – in some hotels. But, of course, we do not want a subtle fragrance, but something really cheap and nasty. I used lavender for my trials because deer don't eat it.

HUMAN URINE

Mentioned earlier as effective against foxes, and I can personally confirm that it will shift deer – a lesson learned on two or three occasions while out stalking! Several correspondents commented. From South Africa: 'One part human urine to ten parts water, sprinkled over the rose bushes will stop deer from eating them. I promise it works – and it's for free! Renew after rain!' From a member of the Women's Institute, no less, signing herself A. N. Oldie. 'Just spend a penny when its dark near area that needs protecting'. From Scotland: 'In a previous house where the deer could only get in at limited places, we found that human urine – supplied by my husband at dead of night – seemed to deter the roe'. (The kilt comes into its own?).

But another lady – keen to try it, as it had been recommended – wrote 'My husband would not co-operate'. Application problems may be a delicate subject, and a large garden might put a strain on resources, but I think future researchers should note the possibilities. Incidentally, several people wrote in to say that deer's urine would actually kill plants, heather being one example. No evidence of cropping with teeth was visible – just the withering.

Visual deterrents

VARIOUS

Great imagination was shown in the choice of visual objects that, it was hoped, might scare away deer. They included plastic toy windmills, strips of aluminium foil and glitter bangs, aluminium foil dishes ('the beans were eaten the next day'), little handbag mirrors ('looked awful and achieved nothing'), and even helium-filled Donald Duck balloons (report awaited – failure anticipated). However, another gardener – and his neighbours – had used the tinfoil strips with some success against roe. One or two reports complained that these had been pulled off by jackdaws and taken to their nests. In the main, none of them really succeeded in protecting any plants, though some were thought to have been of use in temporarily blocking entry points.

PLASTIC BAGS

There were some convincing success stories involving the use of white plastic bags of the thin crinkly type, used by supermarkets and other stores. It was thought important that the bags should be white or have a largely white background. The original tip about plastic bags came from a Highland gamekeeper, but it was also recommended by a Swedish gardener, who had recently lost a whole bed of young yellow roses. He had been told that deer disliked anything *white.*

From an Argyll lady gardener, where the most satisfactory results were achieved, the advice was that the bags should be hung in such a way as to encourage them to rustle in the slightest breeze. As well as *seeing* something unusual in movement, it appeared that the *noise* also frightened the deer. She wrote, 'Even our almost human cats show signs of being unnerved by the sound of the sudden rustling'.

The gardeners who were using the plastic bags all agreed that they looked unsightly, so for their nocturnal raiders, they were put out in the late evening and taken away in the morning. It was no more of a chore than shutting up the chickens at night or taking the dog out for a last walk before bed, and the results were definitely worth it! For just blocking entrance routes that are out of the way, they were mostly left in place.

The flower beds to be protected were surrounded by a single cord, stretched between posts, at 4 ft height, with the bags fastened at intervals along these cords.

The Argyll pioneer – after a successful summer when she picked 'armfuls of roses and summer bedding plant flowers' – had further proof of the efficacy of the system when the frosty weather came, and she was able to see the tracks of the deer in the white rime. They were avoiding the areas of the rustling bags.

My own modest trials – using only one bag at each of three entry points – deterred the fallow for just one week, but it was during last year's severe drought when there were windfall apples on the ground – a welcome source of sweetness and moisture and therefore the conditions were abnormal. Further more, I think I used too few bags, though they rustled obligingly – but not all the time.

SECURITY LIGHTS

The majority of reports said that the lights did *not* frighten off the deer. After some initial shock effect, in most cases not all, the deer became acclimatised to them. Concerning roe, a correspondent noted: 'I see them walking about and feeding – they take no notice'. Many examples were given, such as occurred in a garden right out in the Forest, where the lights went on and illuminated two or three roe busily grazing some plants under a window. They paused for only a minute or so, and then calmly went on with their floodlit feasting. Another correspondent recorded his lights going on at 2 a.m. – activated by two roe. They stayed undisturbed for about eight minutes and then wandered off. Not all wild animals are scared of a light being suddenly switched on. In my garden when I thought I heard some badgers fighting just outside a window (sometimes they are so noisy that they wake us up) I switched on our floodlight. But there on the lawn was a large dog fox, who seemed quite unconcerned. He remained there for a while, and then pottered off to get on with whatever had been occupying him before he had been so rudely spotlighted.

Among the satisfied customers, two reports stated that there was 'less damage in the actual area of the light' and similarly, 'Nothing is now chewed near the house'. A third noted 'less damage this winter – the deer now seem to pass through the garden, without stopping'.

For those with the funds, I would have thought security lights might be worth installing – paying particular attention to the direction of the beams. Even if they do not banish the deer, they will almost certainly provide all sorts of interesting nocturnal wildlife dramas, normally seen only on television.

SCARECROWS OR TATTIE-BOGLES (OR IN HAMPSHIRE – GALLIBAGGERS)

The model I tested is described as a 'wind-powered, constantly revolving scarecrow'. It consists of the image of a life-size man on one side wearing shirt and trousers in different vivid colours, and on the reverse side the predominant colour is *white*, which looks quite ghostly when it moves round at dusk. The structure is so designed in a thin 'S' shaped aerofoil that it revolves in the slightest breeze. The scarecrow is slipped into a solid ground base: two or three of these mountings are probably advisable, so that the scarecrow can surprise the visiting deer from different vantage points, when moved about. The apparatus is extremely well made, and has been developed after some years of research. It has been used on agricultural crops, vineyards,and fish farms among other places. However, at £120 it would probably be expensive for the average gardener.

I installed the scarecrow near the deer's usual entry points, and then moved it to different locations. Flashing red, green and white in the sun, it looked very impressive, but, as I feared, it only kept the deer (my 'regulars') out of the garden for one week. They simply came in from another direction. Subsequently, when I disturbed them, they pronked rather unwillingly past the scarecrow into their usual field. By raking the soil to a fine tilth at their normal entry point, I noted that they did eventually learn to come in past the scarecrow, though not nearly as often as before. Perhaps, when it was not moving? Our one-acre garden has quite a lot of protective cover, so they can find corners where they cannot see the scarecrow. It might be more effective in an open garden with fewer hiding places: and wilder, more peripatetic deer would, I think, avoid coming within a hundred yards of the scarecrow. I tested it for a period of three months during the winter.

(Particulars from Phoenix Agritech UK Ltd, Lower Upton, Little Hereford, Ludlow, Shropshire, SY8 4BB).

Another type of 'scarecrow' – battery-operated and connected to a garden hose – has recently been developed which detects an animal 35 ft away by movement and body heat. A pulse of water spray then jets out for 3 seconds, and allegedly scares the animal greatly. The apparatus can be hidden in foliage so that the deer cannot easily see where the threat comes from. This is said to make the intruder suspicious and avoid the area.

(Particulars from Store More Garden Blds Ltd, Latham Close, Bredbury Ind. Park, Stockport, Cheshire, SK6 2SD).

Sound effects

ULTRASONIC TRANSMITTERS

Phoenix Agritech also make a variety of ultrasonic – and audible – sound deterrents which have been developed for a wide range of purposes, including keeping birds away from airfields, foxes away from lambs, and the protection of soft fruit, arable and other crops.

Below: Usually, only the flowers of Pelargoniums are taken. In this photograph the deer were disturbed halfway through their stripping of the bloom.
Right: Before the deer visit.

Below: Young Camellia defoliated by fallow in Jan - Feb.

Lily buds attacked in July: sometimes they are just sampled and then spat out. Some lily species are rarely touched, while others are prime favourites.

Mature Forsythia frayed and gnawed by fallow in February. Three brittle stems have been snapped off at the base.

Photo: Pamela McGown

This Christmas tree, grown from seed, has been badly frayed by fallow.

Young broom *(Cytisus)* are regularly frayed each winter.

Above Left: Bluebell leaves/shoots are severely cropped in the early spring. The blooms, if they survive to that stage, are usually left alone. Above Right: Typical deer bite on a *Centaurea montana*.

Below: Hyacinths suffer the same fate – bitten down as their shoots emerge, but ignored when they are in bloom (unlike tulips).

To show the positive side of managing gardens with deer problems.

Photo: Ann Stewart

Photo: Norma Chapman

Above: Foxglove (Digitalis) is resistant. Above Right: Snowdrops are resistant to deer. Contrary to appearances, the Muntjac was not eating the snowdrops).

Below: Euphorbias (spurge) are never eaten. *E.wulfenii* are shown at the rear, and *E.polychroma* in the foreground. Narcissi are also always safe.

Photo: P.de Jager and Sons Ltd

Above: Lily-of-the-valley ('Berlin Giant') is resistant.

Left: Peony. *From a correspondent:* 'The deer have eaten almost everything else in the garden: we shall end up with nothing but peonies!'

Below: Rock rose (cistus) is resistant.

Hibiscus are resistant to deer.

Photo: Thompson & Morgan Ltd

Potentilla (White Queen) is resistant.

Lavender is never touched.

Photo: Norfolk Lavender Ltd

Photo: Hillier Nurseries

Photo: Bobby Ely

Above: Buddleias are very resistant. It is encouraging to know that the common 'butterfly bush' is safe from deer.

Left: Christmas rose (*Hellebore niger*) is untouched by deer in the Austrian mountains and similarly avoided in English gardens.

Below: *Mahonia japonica* flowers are occasionally nibbled but suffer minimal damage.

The sounds can be programmed to alter frequencies, direction, duration of transmission, volume and so on. From the way variety can be provided I would think such a device could well keep deer on the move. Concerning the ultrasonic transmitter, used with additional slave units, one successful report has been received regarding its effectiveness against deer. At about £500, it might be an investment for fruit farms, nurseries and so on.

I see no reason why small ultrasonic transmitters should not be developed on the lines of the existing ones that successfully keep rats away from food storage premises. A recent case showed that when the current was accidentally switched off, the rats came back immediately, which is proof of its effectiveness.

TRANSMITTING ANIMAL NOISES
Colonel Blashford Snell, the distinguished explorer, attempted to protect his roses from marauding deer by transmitting recordings of African lions. These were activated by infra-red sensors. Initially, the settings were too sensitive and the recordings were triggered off by cats in the daytime and bats at night. The Colonel reported that the results were better than lion dung, and the roaring 'was indeed terrifying!' However, the deer eventually got used to it, so he then tried howling wolves; but this caused 'a bit of trouble with the nearby Hunt kennels'. Nothing, if not resourceful, but then one would expect that of an explorer.

HUM-LINES
Several gardeners wrote in about hum-lines. These are narrow plastic lines about 5 mm in width and about 100 m in length, which can be stretched on sticks about 4 ft above the ground. The deterrent effect is created by the line making a constantly varying pattern of noise and movement. It is important to read the instructions about getting the line taut and avoiding twists. I found careful setting was necessary to get the line humming. The lines are very inexpensive. Ideally some movement of air is needed to make them work properly, but even on a still day, the manufacturers say they seem to deter bird pests, for which they were originally invented. Sometimes I could detect a slight thrumming, but at other times I could hear nothing though I could see movement in the line. But, the deer have far better hearing then I have.

One lady with a serious fallow deer problem in Essex, reported that she moves her line about the garden as different flower beds or vegetables reach their vulnerable stage. A season or two ago she said it really saved her poppies – oriental, Shirley and opium – for the first time in several years; the deer had already started to bite the buds off. The lines had also been effective in protecting some runner beans and strawberries. Another user had put the lines around some young carrots that were already under attack from muntjac – and the damage ceased, 'But,' said this wise lady 'the best deterrent is still a good fence'.

In my own trials with a hum-line called the Agralan BUZZLINE, I set up a baited area with windfall apples which was probably unfair! Five days later some of the apples had gone, and the next day the line had been snapped. I think this may have frightened the thief, who probably ran off without taking any of the apples on that occasion. I mended the line, set it up again and in three days' time the apples were being taken regularly and the lines left intact. The deer were just going underneath. I shall persevere with the hum-line, probably in combination with something else.

ORANGE TAPE

Years ago I was shown round a traditional walled garden in Belgium by the Head Gardener, complete in green baize apron. Over some of the tender young vegetable crops he had stretched lengths of the familiar orange tape used around road works. This, he assured me, successfully prevented any woodpigeon damage. One or two reports have been received about its successful use against deer.

Animals as deterrents

DOGS

Except in a few circumstances, dogs seem to be of no consequence as a deterrent. Perhaps a single deer – new to raiding gardens – might be put off briefly by the smell of dog's urine or faeces, but this would not last for very long. The failure/success rate was 6 to 1.

One of the very positive reports about dogs being useful as garden wardens concerned some very alert terrier puppies who 'barked and chased about a great deal'. No damage had occurred since the pups arrived. Elsewhere, in an area where ruthless poachers were using long-dogs, the deer had become very jumpy. But for the most part it is a case of dogs being virtually ignored. Some anecdotes will illustrate this failing on the part of man's best friend.

For decades the New Forest rangers have nearly all had beagles, which were used in their deer control work. At one time the hounds lived in outside kennels with a long exercise wire so that they could run up and down. It was quite common to see fresh deer droppings and slot marks close to the kennels made by deer visiting in the night.

Our neighbours who keep a labrador also frequently see droppings within a few feet of the front door, when they open up the house in the morning. Another correspondent has five labradors: 'They watch the roe feeding from their kennels; the roe watch the dogs and feed unconcernedly without any fear at all'. From the same source: 'We have a most boisterous vociferous dog, who does tend to send them packing when they appear, but this does not deter them from coming in again'. And another report of a dog 'confronted by a deer only twenty yards away. The dog barked a lot and stared at the deer. The deer stared back – unmoved'.

One subscriber to the survey has a tame muntjac which shares the quarter-acre garden with his two spaniels, which the muntjac dominates! And there are quite a few reports of dogs, often spaniels, entering a copse and being chased out at high speed by the resident roe! An owner of an 'ancient golden retriever' also recounted how his dog had been sharply ejected from a wood by a defensive roe. In another case a sheltie started to chase some roe, but 'within seconds', wrote the owner: 'he appeared running at top speed with the deer in hot pursuit . . . I ran home to find him totally exhausted at the back gate'. One lady with a sense of humour, wrote and told me that her pet tom cat had *not* succeeded in keeping any deer out of the garden!

SHEEP
A number of reports suggested that deer are uneasy when sheep are nearby. Writing about roe deer, the Duke of Wellington commented: 'They intensely dislike coming into an area in which sheep have been run. I think this may be because the smell is alien to them and one which they not only dislike, but which makes them feel insecure, since the smell of sheep lessens their ability to wind danger'. Other reports confirmed this, including a friend in Hampshire, who had noticed that no roe had entered his garden

since his neighbour had put eight sheep in the field adjoining his boundary fence. And from East Sussex: 'The fallow never visit our "vegetable patch", which contains two hundred vines and fruit trees, as well as vegetables. I really think that it must be because of the rather heavily stocked sheep which graze the fields around it'. On the open uplands, of course, sheep and deer – mostly red deer – will graze over the same area without obvious problems, but the moors are very extensive.

I appreciate that very few gardeners will now rush out and buy some sheep, but I have included the information because it may give us a lead on related possibilities – the smell of sheep grease or sheep droppings. In fact, sheep droppings have been 'recommended' for protecting new plantings of small shrubs. No details available. No information was forthcoming on the subject of goats, though one lady did ask if anyone had tried a llama to keep deer away! Apparently they are strictly territorial, and will see off any fox who dares to try and steal lambs.

Cows

To my surprise, a correspondent wrote: 'Cows seem to be the best deterrent. The (roe) deer look distinctly disconcerted when cows are in the field and appear in our garden less often'. And 'Cattle are put out in the parkland in April, segregated by ordinary electric fencing. The visits from fallow lessen at this time. Is it coincidence?' (In fact, the peak damage does normally begin to ease off at this time). So perhaps there was something in the old Victorian recipe of soot and cowdung paste? (See 'Odds and Ends' on page 70), or the concoction from the USA which included eggs and milk?

A report from scientists at the Macaulay Land-Use Institute stated that penned red deer – maintained for venison production – kept themselves as far away as possible from other farm animals, kicking and butting any that got too close.

When penned next to PIGS they became disturbed.

Geese

A number of people have enquired about deer and geese, suggesting there may be some deterrent effect, but evidence is thin on the ground. Among them, is a friend across the valley, who has a garden full of favourite 'deer plants' (which would never survive in my garden), but in her case the deer never come into her garden. In this instance they are nocturnal raiders. There is no cover nearby for them to dart into, if they sense danger, hence no daytime forays. At night the geese are brought in from an adjacent field, and shut up in their fox- and badger-proof house in the garden. The owner wonders if their smell or their chatter – should they hear or sense something moving about in the garden – scares away the deer. And a note about Canada geese, 'We had these noisy geese descend . . . the fallow did less damage at that time, but I was also using Renardine'.

GUINEAFOWL AND PEAFOWL
An obvious choice as good loud cackling sentries. Only one person wrote in about them and said that in spite of them – about twelve of each – an Irish yew and a young holly close to his house had been eaten down.

Home-made deterrents
Two were sent in from the USA – I was interested to see both contained eggs. From Bob Tanem, an experienced nurseryman in California: 'Combine in a blender two eggs, one cup of skim milk, one cup of water, and a "spreader-sticker". Use as a spray on your plants every 7–14 days. I have found that this works for the entire season'. Bob Tanem agreed that 'mothballs and human hair had some redeeming qualities for short periods of time'. He also mentioned blood meal, which ties in with the strange story that I have quoted earlier.

The other recipe came from Bill Brady in Colorado – much requested by local landowners in a gardening newsletter. 'Two eggs lightly mixed into one cup of water. Just get the eggs in suspension, don't froth it up. Then mix into one gallon of water and spray it thoroughly onto the plants and trees. This should be started early in the spring, before the deer start to browse and get into the habit. It also seems to keep the rabbits, chippies and other similar herbivorous critters away. A light rain will not wash it off, but spray again after any heavy weather. Good luck!'

At least we should be grateful for small mercies – the absence of chipmunks.

From Connecticut yet another eggs-and-water solution to be sprayed on which 'works fairly well in some situations.'

Odds and ends

Ginger root was put forward as a repellent, but no instructions were available as to how it should be used. The same applied to a 'disgusting Victorian remedy', a paste made by mingling soot and cow dung with water. Some people might rather have the deer. In the same genre was pig slurry, sprayed on beside a garden hedge by a Dorset farmer, with a roe invasion on his hands. It was apparently 'totally effective as long as it lasted, but rendered that part of the garden quite uninhabitable'. And in a garden that was badly attacked by roe – *curry powder*. The owner wrote: 'I did, however, have a few weeks' respite when I scattered curry powder around the borders. It kept the cats out too. Of course, you have to do it regularly for full effect'. Finally, another from the USA, 2 tbs of Tabasco in a gallon of water sprayed on every two weeks.

Surfaces walked on by deer

Thinking that deer might feel nervous about walking on certain unusual surfaces – as opposed to grass, leaves, soil etc. – I invited comments. But, nothing underfoot, it seems, will deter them; gravel, brickwork, uneven paving stones, concrete and tarmac were given an 'all clear'. In a Sussex garden the roe habitually walked round the edge of a swimming pool, which often smelled of chlorine, but they didn't seem to object. As to stone steps, deer will happily climb fairly shallow steps to get to terraces where there are flowers in pots, edible shrubs and so on. But I have seen other gardens where the stone steps were fairly steep, and these had never been negotiated.

In one garden an expanse of plastic netting (temporarily removed from the fruit cage) was left on the ground, and it was noticed that the deer refused to cross it. It was then pegged down, but not taut, and it still inhibited the deer from crossing it. At certain times such netting on the ground would probably have to be lifted for grass cutting, soil maintenance etc: it might also look rather untidy or be a slight danger to pets, but it could have possibilities as some sort of 'no-go' corridor. If too narrow, the deer would, jump it. More trials are needed.

Plant barriers

The effectiveness of any physical or off-putting barrier in the form of repellent plants depends on how hungry the deer are, and how desirable the vegetation is behind the protective screen. One correspondent cites a plant *Cimicifuga racemosa* (a bugbane) which was growing wild in a woodland garden, and was about the only thing that the deer never touched. However, other plants that were desirable to the deer and which were surrounded by the bugbane were cropped without hesitation. Other similar reports were received.

Sturdy shrubs – once established – have been successfully used to close entry routes, and to some extent to deter deer from reaching through or over to get at something palatable just beyond. They are worth trying in suitable places. (See note on roses).

CHAPTER SEVEN

FENCES AND OTHER BARRIERS TO DEER

The deer-proof fence

Gardeners under siege are often told to erect a deer-proof fence round their property, and 'that will be the end of the problem'. The advice is sometimes administered in the sort of tone that suggests: 'I don't know what all the fuss is about'. However, the owner of Jasmine Cottage is quite likely to wince at being thus addressed. Proper deer fencing is expensive, and until it weathers or is screened by evergreens, climbers and so on, it can be unsightly. Many correspondents wrote that they couldn't stand the idea of living in a Colditz fortress. Having been a PoW myself, I understand these sentiments. One lady, who had been learning the hard way, and by degrees had installed post-and-rail, chain link, chicken wire and electric fences round her shrinking garden, confessed that it looked more like Steptoe's backyard or Colditz every day!

My postbag is full of reports of fences that failed. There was the muntjac that had scrambled over a 6 ft fence and another that had wriggled underneath: the fallow buck that had been observed working its antlers through a 12 in gap between the wires and then squeezing its body through.

As to jumping, Vezey-Fitzgerald, one time editor of the *Field*, wrote 'Fallow are magnificent jumpers and can easily clear 7 ft.' The stories of deer jumping over 8 ft fences were legion! Frightened deer will, of course, jump much higher obstacles when being chased *out* of a garden, than when seeking entry in their own time. There was the galling episode of the conscientious gardener who always shut his five-barred gate to keep the deer out. In due course he saw a fallow jumping it, and was beside himself with rage. For those who want to consider whether fencing – or part-fencing – might be appropriate for their particular needs, some ideas are put forward.

The construction
If the fence is to be a DIY effort, the handyman must be sure to use netting with the proper mesh size designed for the purpose and install it correctly. Chicken wire or ordinary nylon netting will not do, and may result in animals getting entangled in it and becoming injured. Semi-rigid Netlon is satisfactory. The ground must be levelled, if necessary, with any depressions filled in. The straining posts and the tension of the wires must be suitably adjusted, and the fenceposts at the right distance for the particular weight of wire and the length of the fence. A comprehensive booklet on the subject is published by the Forestry Commission. Bulletin 102 by H. W. Pepper.

If the money is available, I would recommend that deer fencing should be undertaken by a professional who understands the ways of deer. Though all deer are good jumpers, the smaller species really prefer to wriggle underneath or squeeze through chance gaps. Badgers and rabbits will make holes which the deer are delighted to profit by. The bottom of the netting must be securely pegged into the ground. As to fence heights, our local forester keeps it simple: 'Six foot to keep 'em out, and seven foot to keep 'em in'. This is about the height 6.24 ft (1.9 m) used for most enclosures in the New Forest. 6.6 ft (2 m) would be safer for red deer, and although 4.9 ft (1.5 m) is often suggested for roe, the standard 6.2 ft (1.9 m) would be less risky. Roe are agile.

The netting can either be in one piece from top to bottom, strengthened by single wires one-third and two-thirds of the way up, or in two halves laced together at the join. The cheapest is the standard all-in-one netting, with the poles about 8 ft (2.4 m) apart. This is a light-specification fence, which I have had installed alongside part of one boundary and which has been entirely satisfactory. If strengthened with taut high tensile steel wires, the poles can be further apart, and the fence will be less visible. For forestry enclosures and some gardens, a heavy specification is needed. This is the fence in two halves – with the lower half consisting of heavy duty netting such as is used for stock fencing – and the top half of a larger mesh netting, the mesh being graduated and not all the same size.

While planning the deer fencing, it may also be worth thinking about keeping out rabbits, if they are a problem. Ideally, the rabbit netting – with a small mesh of 1.25 ft (38 cm) – should extend about 3 ft (90 cm) above the ground, and be an addition to the deer fence (on the outside). It should be dug in at the bottom. To save money, rabbit netting alone can serve as the bottom half, with the larger mesh netting – either lightweight one-size mesh or the heavier graduated mesh – forming the top section. If this is all of strong construction, with adequate posts and taut wires, it will be quite serviceable, and last for many years.

As to other intruders, a letter to the *Field* magazine from a coffee planter in Southern India asked for ideas on keeping out the antelopes which were raiding his coffee crops. 'Fences of any sort are quite useless' he wrote, 'as they are knocked down by the elephants'. At least in leafy Hampshire we are spared intrusions by clumsy jumbos.

Low cost fence

From the Wyre Forest Nature Reserve comes the recommendation of a well-tried, low cost fence, which the fallow deer simply will not cross. The inventor (manager, John Robinson) describes it as standing at 4.5 ft (1.37 m): oak stakes supporting two strands of barbed wire at the bottom, topped with standard pig netting, inverted so that the small mesh is at the top. He felt this arrangement might help to deter fallow deer from approaching, as it was more visible than normal fencing. This was only supposition, but the fact remained that the deer wouldn't jump it. (The area is an English Nature site).

Wide hedges

Deer will not voluntarily jump over a barrier if they cannot see what lies on the other side. A nearby garden provides a good example. It is full of deer edibles, and surrounded by an old chest-high, evergreen hedge, consisting largely of holly, with some thorn, privet, maple, ivy and other chance inhabitants. The deer never jump over it, because it is both thick and wide – probably 3 ft (90 cm) across. They cannot see where they might land. This hedge is low enough to allow the resident splendid views across the forest: there is no bottled-in feeling (for old Oflag detainees).

In another part of the forest, well-populated with roe and fallow,

I was surprised to see roses flourishing in a garden that was only surrounded by a rather unkempt token hedge about 3.5 ft (1 m) in height, but growing between a double barbed wire fence. The main plants were thorn, briar, bramble, old man's beard, and other bird-sown greenery. The vegetation wasn't very dense, but it was *wide* enough across the top to deter the deer. Height is not everything, which may be important when thinking about the aesthetic side of the problem.

An American gardener described two low fences, erected sufficiently close together with only a narrow strip of grass in between, which the white-tailed deer found too restricting to jump in and out of. This was found to be satisfactory in protecting some public gardens. It would probably take up no more space than a wide hedge. Deer are also nervous about jumping uphill, but conversely will benefit if taking off from higher ground, which may mean that the fence height will have to be increased.

Overhead wire

From Austria, and two or three gardens at home, came the observation that deer do not like to jump over a fence or hedge, if there is anything overhead like a length of wire. The main correspondent (concerned with red and roe in Inverness), having failed with human hair and Renardine, wrote: 'We are in the process of erecting a rose-bower type of fence along one boundary, using rustic larch poles. The netting is only 3 ft (90 cm) high, then there is a gap up to the single overhead wire, which is stretched along the 6 ft (1.8 m) poles.

In another garden they have used two overhead wires, some 6 in apart, and so far the deer have refused to jump through it. There are always exceptions: this one also from Scotland reported: 'A roe was seen leaping between the one-foot spaced wires above a 4 ft (1.2 m) fence'. Magnificent aiming is all one can say!

The rose-bower lady had also successfully used another wire fence only 2.5 ft (76 cm) high. This had wooden supports angled out from the posts at 45° (such as one sees outside high-security establishments) with a couple of strands of barbed wire stretched along the supports. Total height about 3.5 ft (1 m). A low hedge would screen the MOD-type fence for anyone susceptible to the fortress aspect. The lady thoughtfully added that the land on the other side was only rough grazing, and not a 'sensitive' area!

Other visual deterrents

Users of electric fence tapes, as opposed to wires, have expressed the view that this visual extra may add to the effectiveness, rather as the designer of the Wyre Forest fence felt that putting the small mesh at the top made the fence more noticeable. There is no proof either way. A friend is currently trying strips of tin foil wound round the top strands of his wire fence in the hopes of alarming approaching roe at critical times of the year. Not perhaps an enhancing feature for most gardens, but if it works it might be suitable for the back garden, or other out-of-the-way areas. Of course, the silver paper could equally well work against the operator considering how curious deer are about anything new.

The growing rose barrier

In the USA I have seen crash-barriers along the highways, consisting of thick plantings of *Rosa multiflora*. No deer would consider jumping them. I suspect they might be rather uncontrollable, and they could also grow very wide, but I feel there may be some merit in considering impenetrable vegetation.

A correspondent from Brazil mentions a living hedge or belt of the 'pencil tree' (Portuguese name for *Euphorbia tirucalli*) a sort of cactus without prickles, which nothing will pass or even nibble. This is used to keep sundry raiders from crops with complete success.

As already noted, a plantation owner in East Africa whose coffee and pawpaw crops were sometimes plundered by zebras and antelopes, found that thick thuya (*plicata*) hedges were an excellent deterrent: quick growing, available and controllable, but to my mind rather sombre looking.

Following up the living barricade idea, I wrote to David Austin Roses (of Albrighton) to ask if he had any ideas about rose barriers. He listed the following that would certainly grow wide enough to deter deer (and be very decorative): The Garland, Paul's Himalayan Musk, Francis E. Lester, Pink Bouquet, Kew Rambler, Rambling Rector and *R. Eglanteria*.

Cattle grids

In the New Forest, because of the free-ranging ponies, donkeys, and cattle belonging to the commoners – and in the pannage month the pigs let loose for the acorns – many householders have cattle grids to keep the stock out of their gardens. They do not, however, always deter deer. A roe was recently seen leaping over one. They are quite often seen jumping out when being chased, but on this occasion it was jumping in. On balance they are quite effective. It is vital to ensure that any 'wings' on either side of the gateposts are high enough to seal the gaps.

Electric fences

These were the subject of very mixed reactions varying from: 'Totally effective,' to 'The deer got used to them and jumped them'. A nearby gardener, who had been regularly supplying me with useful reports of the misdeeds of her visiting fallow, told me one day that she regretted the flow of data was now at an end. She had finally lost patience and installed an electric fence. However, the following morning when she looked out of her window, there was a buck standing in a flower bed, as usual. It looked at her for a while, and then after she had shouted and waved her arms, it leaped effortlessly over the new fence.

Some people without any experience of electric fences may not realise that when deer are 'in flight', with all four feet off the ground, they are not earthed and therefore escape getting a shock. In any case, their susceptibility to an electric shock is quite different to that of farm stock. A Forestry Commission research team recorded that no visible reaction was observed when a roe deer rubbed its back against an electrified wire. For some time it has been known that the little roe can withstand a much more powerful shock than the larger red deer, and both can withstand a good deal more than us humans.

Whether it worries them or not, deer seem to know when the current fails. Just as cows in a field can tell if water is running through a feed-pipe, even when there is no gurgling discernible to the human ear, so perhaps deer – with their wonderful hearing – can pick up a humming or vibrating inaudible to us. Or do they *sense* electricity running through the wire? Cats are known to 'hear' residual electricity. At all events, when it's off they will take advantage of the fact very quickly. One of a number of correspondents recounted how, by mistake, their current was turned off. They were only alerted to the fact by seeing deer in the garden in no time at all. Up till then they had apparently been effective. Another letter described the skid marks made by a running deer coming to a halt, just before it came into contact with the live wire.

To get the maximum benefit out of an electric fence, all equipment must be properly installed and regularly serviced. Herbage will grow up and can short the power supply, branches can fall down and rupture the wire: this can also be done by the deer. Routine inspections are essential. Early June is the best time to check the weed growth with a strimmer. Herbicides are sometimes recommended for 'burning' down the grass, but this leaves an unsightly dead brown strip along the fence. For battery-operated models a tester is essential.

Many types of electric fence are in use: most have some limitations and it would be difficult to recommend a 'best buy' for all situations. One discouraging correspondent made the point: 'The fence acted as a deterrent for a while, until the adults learned to step over it and the young to walk under it'. (This must have been a single strand fence). Certainly, two strands are better than one, and three are better than two. Suggested heights used by someone who succeeded in protecting his vegetable garden from fallow were 18 in (45 cm), 3 ft (90 cm) and 4.5 ft (1.4 m). Other satisfactory fences used against roe and muntjac used three strands, the top one being 4 ft (1.2 m) high.

Reports were received of vulnerable woodlands, where damage was occurring, being successfully protected when tapes, as opposed to wires, were put into use. A double strand of wide tape also proved successful against roe in a large Sussex garden. This was, however, part of a well-keepered estate, where the deer management and culling were of the highest order. Metallic tape, which is the most visible, is also available.

CHAPTER EIGHT

PROTECTING INDIVIDUAL PLANTS

Shrub shelters, tree guards etc.

'Needs protection when young,' was regularly advised for certain plants. These come in two categories. First, as already mentioned, deer are prone to harry anything new – even an established plant moved to a new position – and then they can get bored with it. Attacks vary from nibbling to pulling a plant right out of the ground, and occasionally eating it down to soil level. The second category includes shrubs which will, after the novelty has worn off, in any case become less edible as they mature. The original young, tender shoots will toughen up: the plant will grow taller and sturdier, and the deer will then tend to leave them alone.

Even some roses (like *rugosas*, English roses, and R. *glauca* – mentioned by one correspondent) will excite less and less interest as they grow older. The climbers will, of course, eventually grow above nibbling height and bloom well. Some of the cotoneasters, which are not favourites, can suffer badly when young, but are later completely ignored. (*C. simonsii* was cited as one).

All these plants need only short-term protection, while they are establishing themselves. Some will suffer from an occasional fall from grace and undergo 'an annual deer prune', as someone put it, but nothing very serious. I would accept this slight irritation, rather than continue with wire netting defences.

Home-made protective devices
Luckily, though I have had more than my fair share of deer damage, I have not needed to buy any special tree or shrub guards. I keep a

79

roll of sturdy, green plastic-coated netting in the garden shed, and make up tubes or aprons of various shapes and sizes, as required. A lavender hedge has been rescued from constant trampling by erecting a strip of netting behind the bushes, which was the direction whence came the heavy-hoofed approach. The deer now stop and jump over. The netting is only the same height as the lavender and is practically invisible.

From Dorset, a lady who was much troubled by sika, sent me some photographs of her herbaceous borders in which those plants that were vulnerable were protected by cylinders of 3 ft (90 cm) high green 'clematis' netting. These blended in well with all the other surrounding vegetation, and much of the protective netting was hidden by the plants in front. The overall effect was good. She mentioned that she also grew sweet peas against the netting, which in her case remained uneaten. (I suspect mine would be demolished!). No trampling was reported.

A new *Robinia pseudoacacia* is typical of the few ornamental trees that I have planted and which need protection. The side shoots that protruded through the wire netting sleeve have been bitten off, but I am not too concerned about that. With netting, as opposed to a solid plastic tree shelter, it was to be expected: the rest is growing well. Where it is sited, I thought a tall plastic cylinder would look too unsightly.

There are others that are an awkward shape to protect when young, such as certain hydrangeas, which get 'topped' in my garden, though they are ignored in others. I would need a relatively large covering of netting if a young hydrangea was to be completely covered. So here I just have to use my secateurs to tidy up the haphazard pruning by the deer. In time they leave the plants alone.

Most gardeners make up their own cages, arches or tunnels of netting which suit low-growing plants. When the foliage grows through, it is often eaten, but at least the plant itself survives. Some comment that these netting-covers seem to deter the deer from approaching the plants underneath. Wire micro-cages 3 in × 10 in × 6 in (7.6 cm × 25.4 cm × 15.2 cm) are available from Link-Stakes of Daventry. Badly barked tree trunks can be effectively protected and given a chance to recover by encasing them *loosely* in chicken wire up to a height of 5.6 ft (1.7 m).

One or two writers confessed to 'tossing a bit of netting over plants like camellias at a vulnerable time', as a useful anti-deer measure. Remembering my failures with similar efforts designed to outwit the blackbirds that were intent on stripping my currants, and loathe to accept the problem of unravelling a tangle of netting after a windy night, I desisted for a while. However, some trials with squares of green small-mesh netting and fishing weights hung at all four corners – also on camellia bushes – seemed to work quite well. They were removed just before flowering.

Another gardener covers her 'particular treasures' every night with garden fleece, which shows the lengths to which some people will go to protect their plants. She describes this crepuscular duty as 'tedious, but worthwhile'. I admire her dedication. I had an elderly aunt who experienced a similar deep joy for certain close friends in her plant world. 'Come and see my so-and-sos' invariably meant a trek round to the back of the shrubbery, and there in an out-of-the-way place she would persuade me to kneel down and admire some tiny bloom, poking out of a scattering of dead leaves or perhaps from under a granite boulder. Over the years, I have learned not to ask 'Is it scented?', and spoil the pleasure of the person concerned; for how awful it would be if she had to say, 'No, I'm afraid it isn't'.

I realise with some shame that I am obviously not a *real* gardener. I just like picking the first summer bunch of sweet peas, or boasting to some lunch guest that the greengages were from our very own trees. These ordinary pleasures are a million miles away from the insignificant, but much loved rock plant in its secret place.

Commercially available tree guards etc

There is a wide selection of tree shelters on the market, usually made of polypropylene – and tree guards made of Netlon or galvanised wire mesh. The former encase the whole sapling in the tube (round or square; coloured brown, olive green, or 'natural') allowing the young foliage to grow out of the top.

The mesh guards allow side shoots to poke out through the holes, where they may be bitten off, as in the case of my acacia. The diameters vary from 3.33 in (8.4 cm) to 4.5 in (11.4 cm). More spacious shrub shelters up to 8.5 in (21.5 cm) across, are also available (from firms like Tubex of Woking). The nursery that supplies you with your plants will be the best people to advise you which type of guard you need.

It is essential to stake your tubes or cages really firmly: they can get blown over by strong winds, and deer will also push them over. Bucks will sometimes fray or rub against them, as well as chewing off the strap that holds the tube to the sapling. Sometimes they will chew the tube itself. The stakes should be positioned on the windward side and hammered in to the hole before planting the young tree, to avoid damaging the roots. Plastic spiral guards are useless against deer.

The supplier of your tree-guards will need to know which deer are prevalent in your area, so that you get tubes of the right height. For red deer 5.9 ft (1.8 m) is advised: for fallow and sika 5.24 ft (1.6m) for roe and muntjac 4 ft (1.2 m). If the foliage growing out of the top can be reached by the deer, the device illustrated on p??? will soon stop them.

When the sika started to eat off the emerging greenery on the Duke of Abercorn's estate in County Tyrone, Edward Deane, the Head Forester quickly devised a spiked 'crown' to be fitted to the top of each tube. This was cut from a roll of Intermesh. The nibbling ceased abruptly when the deers' noses came into contact with the spikes. About 180 protective 'tops' can be cut from a 50 m roll of Intermesh, available from Stanton Hope of Basildon, Essex. Individual tops are not at present available, but smaller rolls of similar wire mesh netting are probably available at most agricultural merchants. The Forestry Commission publish an illustrated handbook on the subject entitled, 'Tree shelters' Ref HB 07.

CHAPTER NINE

MAINTAINING A DEER-RESISTANT GARDEN

Defensive tactics

Unless a garden is turned into a veritable fortress, a few deer are likely to come in and prospect from time to time. If they find little to their taste, or their favourite plants are well protected, they will probably move on. But if the garden is well stocked with appetising vegetation, it could suffer badly. A single deer can do a lot of damage in one night.

To minimise possible damage, some changes to the old care-free days of deer-free gardening will have to be adopted. They include:

- (1) forming a small informal group of neighbouring gardeners, who are also suffering from deer raids, to co-operate in anti-deer measures.
- (2) asking the owners of any nearby land, who may be responsible for sheltering the invading deer, if they would effect some degree of control. (An invitation to drinks and a view of mangled shrubs and cropped flowers has been known to get some culling started).
- (3) using every means available to make the garden boundaries difficult for the deer to negotiate.
- (4) using deterrents on a trial-and-error-basis, and protecting all new plantings for a period.

Selecting safer varieties

If these measures fail and your garden continues to suffer, you will have no alternative but to rationalise your existing choice of plants:

i.e. abandon your rose beds and whatever else is frequently targeted, and replace them with deer resistant varieties.

As the project has unfolded and I have discussed the selection of less palatable species with other gardeners, I have been heartened to discover how many there are that, for some reason, the deer dislike. I have often walked round the gardens of fellow-sufferers and been told: 'The deer don't seem to eat that'. This would usually refer to lesser-known plants, not obvious safe plants such as peonies or lavender.

As a result, I have tried out twenty or thirty new plants in my deer-infested garden. Admittedly some were a total failure, some were nibbled half-heartedly, but many were untouched. Obviously, it has been sad to discard old favourites and replace them with unfamiliar plants, but at least the garden is surviving and attractive in a different sort of way. Perhaps I had been too conservative in my tastes or too set in my ways? I had always felt that a garden had to have masses of wallflowers and tulips in the spring, and lupins, delphiniums, Canterbury Bells, stocks, snapdragons, borage (for the Pimms), Sweet Williams and so on in the summer. Hollyhocks – even accepting their unsightly rust – were traditional and therefore essential; as were clove-scented pinks sprouting from every corner, and of course, sweet peas. If these flowers were not present in profusion, in my opinion, it wasn't a proper garden! Unfortunately, over half the above plants are on the deer's edible list. Luckily, other old favourites like buddleias, lilacs and laburnums were survivors.

Among my many new acquisitions, that I had never really noticed before in other gardens, was *Choisya ternata*. I wondered why I had not tried it before. They bloom profusely and their foliage, whether green or yellow, is bright and glossy. Their fragrance, so the catalogues tell us, resembles that of orange blossom. This is perhaps going a bit far, but it reminds me of a plant that used to scent the warm humid air of our compound in India, so it is most welcome. And it is deer-proof.

Shrubs

I think it was the word 'shrub', and even worse 'shrubbery', that put me off a whole range of beautiful plants. A shrubbery in my childhood had sinister connotations. I seemed to remember vistas of dark green vegetation, with a bitter, musty smell, and old ivy-covered walls, alive with spiders and drab little moths. The gloomy shed at the end of the shrubbery was where Cook was supposed to dally with the milkman! There was no colour: no honeyed scents; nothing to pick.

How unadventurous I was not to have explored the fascinating world of shrubs. Understandably, when seen in an urban park beside iron railings and tarmac paths, they lose some of their appeal, but as a backdrop to flowers, or as specimen plants in terracotta pots, or in varied groups, they demand attention. Many are deer-proof, though some – like the spotted laurel (*A. japonica*) – which looks bitter and leathery, can be chewed to pieces *when young*. Solitary plants are usually the ones in danger: a laurel hedge, though it may be deer-pruned, will suffer no lasting harm.

Variegated foliage

When re-designing the compromise garden, it is also worth thinking about plants with variegated foliage. In my search for colours, I had neglected them. They can provide every shade of green from sage to holly tones, with highlights of cream and gold. Among the lower orders, the inedible variegated *helichrysums*, the pineapple mints, the bi-colour sages and many others are all an asset in patio pots or as edgings if kept under control. (Variegated ivies often get eaten).

Cushions of colour can also be provided by clumps of low-growing plants such as variegated periwinkles (*Vincas*). Deer may graze them slightly but this does little harm. The larger periwinkle, with its vivid blue flowers, is virtually deer-proof when established. Golden oregano is never eaten, and lady's mantle (*Alchemilla*) – an attractive space filler – is rarely touched. Noses are often turned up at the Hypericums, but their brilliant yellow flowers are worth consideration in a garden under pressure. They are indestructible from any quarter – deer, rabbit, slug or sawfly, as far as I know.

These are merely some common examples of carpeting or filling-in plants that are survivors.

Inexperienced gardeners should remember that some cover plants can become smother plants. I rue the day when I accepted a small piece of *Lamium* from a well-meaning friend. It has now taken over most of the garden.

Replacing casualty plants

In a situation where the occasional deer continues to raid a garden and strike down odd plants here and there (or where deer damage is fairly regular) I have found it a good insurance policy to keep some potted spares to fill any gaps that appear suddenly. This plan has been particularly successful on a small terrace just outside our French windows, where everything is portable. According to the season, we make up a different display in containers: any plastic pots are hidden behind the earthenware ones. In the spring we usually have a few evergreen shrubs like bay, spotted laurel, golden *lonicera* etc. – whatever blends in. These are the back-up cover to containers full of daffodils and narcissi. Surprisingly, we have got away with tubs of wallflowers interplanted with tulips, kept in our safe zone until in bud, and then protected with an apron of neat green plastic netting in front, large mesh and hardly visible. The deer could reach over, but for two years they have not done so.

It is surprising what can be grown successfully in large pots, provided they are properly maintained. Ever since I saw a tall wisteria, covered in bloom, rising from a soil-filled chimney pot in a London basement, I have become a pot addict. One has only to walk round some of the smarter areas in a town to see how adventurous people have become in their choice of flowers and greenery for tubs and even shady courtyards.

At the other end of the scale is the simplicity and tranquillity of the Greek peasant's 'garden'. Apart from one or two huge oleanders and a vine over the porch, there is little else but half a dozen metal oil drums, cut down to size and painted in various colours: whatever has been left over from doing the boat or the cart. These are usually filled with the brightest pelargoniums and look wonderful against the baked soil. They thrive on washing-up water. Anything else would probably be considered overdoing it!

In my collection of spare plants I always keep a number of scented lilies, as well as batteries of smallish pelargoniums, fuchsias and the like, and foliage plants for the front row. With these I can fill any gap, if and when it appears. Lilies are not absolutely immune from attack, but they usually survive: a supporting bamboo or green metal rod can help to deter the deer. I try to keep specimens of different sizes, but I find the most useful are the lilies, as singles, or three to a pot. According to the variety they have a long flowering season.

Not so much in use as spares, but more as seasonal alternatives, I find that *pyracanthas* and *berberis* (particularly *B. darwinii*) – until they eventually become too large – can take a turn and provide some dazzling colours. Some spares such as the single lilies, can also be used to fill spaces in flower borders as well as on terraces, the pots, of course, being buried. Almost anything tall and slim can be used in this slight subterfuge.

Hanging baskets
Hanging baskets can provide a safe display, though one correspondent reported deer standing on their back legs to chew off the trailing greenery. Another deer wrenched down a birds' peanut-feeder, which had been hung in an apple tree to prevent the sparrowhawks knocking off the birds at the feeding table.

In commuter-land I think that some of the 'olde worlde' containers that tend to accompany the hanging baskets look a little out of place i.e. the wheelbarrow full of pelargoniums, lobelia and alyssum; the cartwheel on the ground striving to look natural with the spokes dividing up the herb compartments: the brick well, with bucket and chain, but no water and floral companions. They are also just the right height for the deer.

The gardener who originally wrote to remind me that hanging baskets were worth a mention, as being too high for the deer to reach, said his were satisfactory, though they sometimes got 'troglodyted' by nesting wrens! Another plus for the bird life.

Fenced-off safe zones
Earlier, I mentioned our small deer-proof enclosure, where we grow roses and sweet peas for cutting, among a few other plants essential to my welfare. This is where most of the spare plants in pots are kept until needed, or until they come into bloom. I omitted to say that unlike a fruit cage, no roof is required, which cuts down the price considerably and makes working conditions easier. Even a small wired-in enclosure can be very productive.

Patios
Regarding deer raiding patios, I have had several letters saying how relatively common this is. No doubt the raised height of the plants to nose level constitutes an added bonus for the deer. A typical tale of woe came from a lady gardener, not long retired from a working life spent in a town. She described, as many others have done, the thrill that she and her husband experienced at seeing her first roe deer munching away at a tub of bright winter pansies just outside

their sitting room window. She confessed that the pretty creature, shining wet nose and all, was instantly forgiven for the damage it was doing. In due course, as they watched, it cleared the tub of pansies and left. But by the next morning the mood at Rose Cottage had changed, for during the night, the roe had returned and completely stripped every pansy in every one of four tubs, leaving nothing but a bare and desolate patio, with a few dying plants scattered here and there across the paving stones.

The anecdote at Rose Cottage raises two points. First, new to the ways of deer the owner had unknowingly planted one of the roe's most favourite food items at a hungry time of the year. And second, she was offering a feast of choice pansies – and only pansies – when a mixture of plants might have had less dire results. Of course, mixtures are less spectacular, but in my experience – according to what is planted, the deer will rarely destroy everything in a single tub in one visit. They will usually pick out a favourite first: say, some trailing ivy around the edge and a single petunia. Then a few days later they will perhaps come back for another sample of something edible, but less tempting. In my case, the second visit disposed of some dwarf dahlias, and a gazania pulled out and left on the ground. Some time later they can back again, and nibbled something else, but over half the plants were left. These included some white marguerites and feverfew, some African marigolds, and some pelargoniums. Five tubs were on display – all planted up with mixed flowers. Two containers on either side of the front door, had been planted up with pure salmon-coloured pelargoniums, and these were never touched. A few yards away, next to the mixed tubs of flowers, was a one of red pelargoniums in which half the flowers had been cropped. Perhaps the animal had been disturbed in mid-feast?

I fear that my experiences over the three years did not teach me anything, except that with my spare plants I was able – as the raids continued over a period – to plant up the gaps immediately. So at no time did we have any half empty tubs. In time I shall learn which plants in my particular situation are more or less deer-resistant. And apart from the tubs of pure pelargoniums, which I shall continue to risk, I will not plant out single species. I notice that busy lizzies are often used on their own. In some areas they are a favourite of deer, and in others they do not seem to be touched – at the time of the reports coming in. One lady reported a contented rabbit dozing or sunning itself in a tub of buzy lizzies!

Petunias sometimes escape attack, but not always. A conscientious lady rang me up to say that she had put petunias on the 'never touched' list, but after three years of the deer ignoring them, a whole stone trough of them had been cleared over night.

An amusing incident arose during the patio hostilities.

On one occasion, more as a joke than a serious trial, to fill a gap I 'planted' an artificial white daisy or two, made of some kind of cloth. They were very realistic. Some guests were arriving for a few days and I couldn't find the time to attend to the tubs properly. Neither the guests nor the deer noticed the deception. Within a day or two a deer – and it may have been a young one – pulled the white flowers out and left them on the ground. I don't know what this teaches us about their sense of smell or taste!

CHAPTER TEN

ROSES AND DEER: AN APPRAISAL OF THE PROBLEM

Roses are acknowledged to be the favourites of all deer and many gardeners, so it seems appropriate to discuss the problem briefly, even though nothing very positive has emerged from the hundreds of comments received. Recommendations are thin on the ground. The situation could be summed up by one typical quote: 'My great distress is roses. I've had to dig them all up. I grow dahlias instead – deer don't touch them'. Unfortunately, in some areas dahlias *are* sometimes eaten, though they would not be a first choice.

One lady, invaded by muntjac, told me that she had over twenty rose bushes and had not picked a single bloom for three seasons! Her patience and optimism, no doubt waiting for some miracle cure to be found, amazed me. Another lady, with a hundred strong, healthy rose bushes and eight climbers, planted in the pre-deer era, wrote that after three seasons of severe roe damage, most of her bush roses had been so badly cropped that they had become weak and spindly, and the majority had eventually died. The climbers had survived, but they were bare from the ground up to deer nose height – a familiar story.

Most of the damage to roses occurs just before bud burst: every part of the plant is eaten including the early tender shoots, the mature leaves, the buds and the flowers, The worst harm occurs after a concentrated fertiliser application. Roses clearly have a special attraction for deer, because they are voraciously eaten in mid-summer, when there is plenty of other food available. Correspondents found this particularly galling.

With regard to climbing roses, many wrote of specimens that had become 'bare'. . . 'gawky' and 'eaten to sticks lower down, but with lovely flowers above'. However, a leafless lower storey need not be too much of a problem, because it can often be screened by deer resistant plants in front. One keen gardener showed me her 'New Dawn' growing up the sides of an arch and flowering profusely from 5 ft (1.53 m) upwards. The lower stems had been encircled with netting and camouflaged by a couple of strong clematises. These had obligingly twined up the wooden structure and mingled with the rose blooms. The clematis side shoots were sometimes nibbled, but this minor damage had not prevented the main stems from growing away well and flowering freely higher up. Elsewhere, damage to the lower stems of climbers – when unprotected – was often severe enough to reduce the flowering considerably. But this effect was in the minority.

Ramblers and climbers that will grow up into trees are worth considering. Already mentioned is our Paul's Himalayan Musk which reaches up to the first floor windows and is a sheet of pale pink in mid-summer. It is skirted by a thick circle of protective rhododendrons. Another which blooms well at the top of a tangle of tall shrubs is Raubritter, described in my catalogue as growing to a height of 5 ft, but our specimen blooms profusely at about 12 ft. And in a nearby garden the Rambling Rector flowers well at the top of a tall tree. I have also seen Kiftsgate flowering in trees, and Pink Perpétue, Zéphirine Drouhin, Mermaid, Wedding Day and many others. The beautiful Constance Spry, spectacularly displayed at Mottisfont Abbey where it is grown as a climber – will also attain a respectable height and spread. In all cases the plants must obviously be protected when young, and the base kept caged or screened as they develop.

There is a vast selection of tree climbers, and most nurseries provide lists of roses in this category. Other lists include varieties that are ideal for cutting – should you be considering my 'fruit cage' approach. One can grow thirty to forty roses in a relatively small enclosure, depending on the varieties selected. Admittedly, it may not be quite the same as having colourful beds of roses that are visible from every window, but I can only say that after five barren years the joy of picking our first bunch of roses grown in the 'fruit cage' was intense!

A vase of, say, classic dark red roses – long-stemmed, perfect in shape, uniform and elegant – is wonderful to look at in its own formal way. But it has the 'florist look' about it.

A vase of mixed roses of all colours, shapes and sizes, and probably scented, has obviously come from a garden. Both, in their different ways, have their own special appeal, but to me the garden roses bring the greater warmth to a room.

Many correspondents wrote to say that some roses were more prone to attack than others. For example, my prickly little Burnet roses are never sampled. (I liked the comment from someone: 'I planted *R. pimpinellifolia*, i.e. Burnet roses, and they were untouched, but so boring that deer are welcome to them!'). Where Burnet roses are eaten, the pale lemon Dunwich rose seems to be the least palatable.

Here and there, moss roses were ignored, but this bonus was not universal. The least attractive to deer were undoubtedly mature rugosas. There were many reports on this, such as: 'Rugosas survive quite well, once protected initially', 'I grow mostly rugosas, which the deer leave alone' and so on. (The hips are often popular with deer). Obviously, if a garden contains only one or two rugosas, they stand a chance of being eaten, but if there are great clumps of them they will more likely be ignored. I visited a garden in Dorset, where the heavy roe population was inflicting severe damage on almost everything. But there was a hedge of pink rugosas, from which never a leaf tip was ever taken.

These are, of course, 'majority verdicts'. A few gardeners reported that their Roseraie de l'Hay bushes – as well as other rugosas – had been stripped. And while *Scabrosa* is usually low in the palatability stakes, in one Scottish garden a hedge of this species has been devastated by roe. Nevertheless, rugosas still remain the best option.

A number of defensive measures to protect rose beds were put forward. Although some were successful in one garden, predictably the same idea would fail in another. As an example, a large rose bed was enclosed in wire netting, well weathered and not very noticeable, this kept the invading deer (roe and fallow) at bay. The owner suggested that perhaps they didn't like the feel of the top wire touching their necks. But when another gardener tried the same thing, he found that the netting kept back the roe, but the taller deer just leaned over and cropped whatever was in reach. If really tempted, I think a roe might jump over and eat his fill, unless the bed was very narrow.

Perhaps the most original protective technique that apparently worked consisted of rose beds being underplanted with brambles. These were sunk in large tins to restrict the invasive root growth. Each rose was surrounded with chicken wire, which the brambles soon hid from view. The young brambles looked not unlike rose leaves, and the end result was quite pleasing. The original idea was to hide the bare stems of the roses, but it also deterred the deer. The informant commented that 'the deer were not keen on brambles as they could get them anywhere, so they moved on'. I feel this could be risky because brambles are, in fact, a favourite food of deer in the wild. I would also think that the brambles might cause some cultivation problems: and extra nutrients would have to be provided for the roses. I have included this idea – though it may be chancy elsewhere – because others may adopt the fundamental principles, but alter the detail to fit in with local requirements. Unpalatable foxgloves are sometimes grown in rosebeds – also tobacco – and these would help to hide the netting. And should the roses be attacked, at least the foxgloves will provide a show of sorts.

The best deterrent so far suggested has probably been the rustling white plastic bags, put out at night on a line round the rose beds. But there is room for an extensive armoury of deterrents to suit every contingency!

As to why deer will sometimes ignore one or two roses in a bed and eat all the others remains a mystery: but it is sometimes reported. One grower listed eight different varieties in a bed which were eaten by muntjac, but one -Mme Hardy, the beautiful white damask rose was avoided! It can grow quite tall and be 'whippy', but I expect there were other equally tall bushes in the same bed. A few other reports cited the same occurrence: one or two varieties avoided in a mixed bed – and seemingly no common denominators. It would be pointless to name all the untouched roses because deer do not follow any rules for any length of time. Mme Hardy has a lemony fragrance, but I doubt that the scent has anything to do with keeping the deer at bay. (My informant did not say at what stage the nearby roses were being eaten, i.e. before blooming and scenting, or when in flower).

Another correspondent reported that a mature *Félicité et Perpétue* was never touched. David Austin's handbook describes this rose as having a 'delicate primrose fragrance', and deer do not eat primroses. But I think this is stretching things too far! His descriptions of the various rose scents are intriguing. They include raspberries, myrrh, 'fruity', clove, sharp apple fragrance, peony and so on. Some rose foliage (like *R. Eglanteria*) 'is notable for the strong fragrance of its foliage, which on a warm moist evening will fill a garden'. I had not thought of rose leaves as being a source of fragrance. But, I have strayed away from the basic question – why deer avoid certain roses. It is unlikely that they would be consistent: probably in a couple of years different species would be on the privileged list.

CHAPTER ELEVEN

HERBS, VEGETABLES, FRUIT AND FRUIT TREES, TREES – INCLUDING ORNAMENTAL SPECIES

Herbs

Most herbs are avoided by deer, though an individual animal will sometimes undertake a little sampling. Occasionally, this leads to wholesale feasting.

Angelica.   No reports of being eaten.
Basil.   Though usually a window-sill plant, reported safe when potted plants put out in the garden.
Betony.   (*Stachys officinalis* as opposed to *S. byzantina* or Lamb's Tongue) not eaten (single report).
Chives.   Green shoots quite safe, (also **garlic** shoots), but pink flowers sometimes cropped.
Comfrey.   The occasional nibble.
Coriander.   No reports from gardeners, but when 0.6 ha was grown on a commercial scale, the crop was 'demolished'.
Fennel.   (Common and golden) untouched in several gardens.
Feverfew.   Many reports of it being resistant, though some muntjac in confinement would eat it.
Marjoram and related **Oregano.**   Not touched, except for a single report of roe eating the former.
Mint.   Common, ginger or pineapple, and other varieties never eaten, but in a small garden plot where tame muntjac were kept,

apple and water mint were wiped out. (The only example of mint being eaten.)

Parsley.   Curly and flat-leaf produced a number of safe reports, but the commercial grower of coriander, also lost a crop of parsley to deer. In the Author's garden, some flat-leaf parsley was lightly grazed in mid-summer, but rabbits might have done this, though deer slots were visible close-by.

Rue.   (The herb of Grace – once used for sprinkling Holy water before High Mass). Resistant: toxic if taken internally.

Sage and Tarragon.   No damage reports received.

Sweet Cicely.   Resistant.

Thyme.   A great many reports of it being totally resistant, but a couple of records of plants being eaten in areas where no rabbits were present.

Vegetables

Nearly all vegetables – except members of the **onion family**, including **leeks** and **shallots** – are eaten by deer with differing degrees of intensity. Almost anything that is green and fresh in the vegetable garden is likely to be enjoyed, but there do seem to be distinct favourites. Some correspondents wrote to say that they had had to give up growing certain vegetables, because they were always eaten down. Others grew selected vegetables in netting cages. One commented: 'Our deer are nocturnal raiders and we see their hoof marks all around the cage, as though they were desperately trying to break in!'.

Muntjac are in a slightly different category owing to their smaller jaw opening capacity. The muntjac expert, Norma Chapman, who keeps tame ones for observation, concluded after trials with a carrot, that a circumference of 4.3 in (11 cm) was about the maximum they could cope with. This only concerns root vegetables: they have no problems when grazing, say, carrot tops or spinach leaves.

In order of vulnerability, **runner beans** came out well ahead of all the others as a clear favourite. This puzzled me because **dwarf French beans** growing at a more convenient height, scored only one quarter of the edibility points, compared with the runners. **Broad beans**, with their tougher leaves and pods had about the same rating, and in some gardens were never touched. **Beetroot**

- for deer damaged gardens

Right: 'This area is heavily 'bagged' during the flowering (and budding) season', writes a Scottish correspondent.

Below: 'These crinkly white plastic bags rustle in the slightest breeze and deter roe very effectively. The bags can equally be cut up into strips. There is never any danger to the roses, or other border plants. These roe are nocturnal, so the bags are put out at night and taken in during the day.'

Photo: Maureen Gray

Photo: Maureen Gray

Right: This anti-deer spiked collar devised by Edward Deane, Head Forester, Abercorn Estates, Northern Ireland, ended damage by Sika.

Below: The tulips, and later other vulnerable plants, were protected by a hastily erected screen of plastic netting. Later versions were neater.
Before they were used, various plants were eaten, in spite of being just outside the windows. The fallow were able to reach over the top of the netting, but didn't.

Opposite Top: Climbing rose (New Dawn) with base protected by green netting, camouflaged by Ville de Lyon Clematises (survivors in this garden). Heavy roe population.

Opposite Middle: Lightweight scarecrow revolving in the slightest breeze, revealing coloured reverse side: suitable for fruit crops, nurseries etc. (see text)

Opposite Bottom: Human hair - preferably men's - hung about the roses in muslin bags. Double the amount shown in the picture would be preferable, and regular renewing is essential.

Photo: Robert Scott

Photo: Pamela McGown

Hum-line in position. *P. orientalis* are normally eaten in bud. In contrast, peonies and red-hot poker are never eaten in bud.

Photo: Mrs J. Sims

One metre-wide netting around selected plants. In this garden, sweet peas are grown up some of the netting sleeves which luckily have not been touched, unlike their fate in the author's garden. The front of the border shows Creeping Jenny, Alchemilla untouched, and Asphodels at the back.

Chives are immune from attack, apart from the flowers which are occasionally eaten. They are good nectar-producers for butterflies (see Painted Lady).

Variegated sage (and variegated mint) is resistant.

Herbs such as thyme, are rarely eaten.

Feverfew is resistant to deer.

Photo: Forestry Commission

Above: A Forestry Commission deer-and-rabbit proof fence.

Below: These wide (double) hedges – only five feet high, but five feet across – are never jumped by deer.

tops came next: if the deer pulled hard at them and the beets came out of the ground, they were greedily gobbled up. Deer have a sweet tooth. All parts of the beet are fancied. As one correspondent put it: 'The moment they put their heads above ground, they are attacked'. The third favourite was **spinach**: (few reports separated the annual spinach from the beet variety). Not far behind were **potatoes** – occasionally only the flowers: often the foliage when young (*any* foliage in hungry weather), and the tubers when left on the ground at harvesting time.

Carrots – mostly just the tops – were in the same category: and the **cabbage family**, including **kale** and **purple sprouting broccoli**, were not far behind. There were almost as many reports of **brassicas** being left entirely untouched, (or 'the pigeons have them'), as there were of them being eaten by deer. One report said 'Deer dislike all **brassicas**', but Norma Chapman recorded, '150 **brassicas** being planted one day and all scoffed by muntjac the following night'. The age of the plant would naturally have a bearing on it.

Maize or sweetcorn was quite often eaten down. In some cases it was the growing stems and the green shoots: in others, the corn was trampled down when the cobs were just ripe. These were then eaten – or large parts of them – on the ground. Deer can also be troublesome on the edge of farmers' **maize** fields. In one instance the local deer acquired the taste for maize from the nearby fields, and within a year or two were eating the sweetcorn in a neighbouring garden.

Lettuce, which most people would regard as succulent, was certainly taken from time to time, but as one writer put it: 'With less enthusiasm than one might expect'. One gourmet deer just took out the hearts! **Peas**, for some reason, featured towards the less popular end of the list, along with the **broad beans** already mentioned.

In a number of gardens root vegetables like **swedes, turnips and parsnips** almost escaped attention, with only the tops being grazed occasionally. One tame muntjac, on being offered a parsnip refused it, but among Norma Chapman's animals they were very popular. On one occasion a muntjac became very drunk when the parsnip sugar fermented rapidly in the rumen: it was frosty weather. Temperature control has now been instituted! In fields of roots, deer can be very destructive – just taking a bite out of a swede or turnip, then moving on to the next one.

On the whole the **marrow family (including courgettes)** escaped attention. In my own garden they were untouched for five successive years, until a drought period, when for the first time the fallow ate every part of the plants. Another gardener wrote that his deer ate a few **courgette** buds 'probably out of curiosity', and later started to munch holes in the courgettes themselves. But this was not common. Mine, along with **squashes**, have been untouched since the very dry spell.

In the 'odds and ends' list, there were a few reports of both types of **artichokes** being occasionally sampled: as were **celery, sea kale, cucumber and tomatoes**. Regarding the latter, a muntjac owner confessed to his tame animal being allowed into the greenhouse where he helped himself! A report from the USA said that the situation was very variable. 'Sometimes they (white-tailed deer) went mad and ate off all **tomatoes** and leaves'. Finally, **asparagus**. Not a lot of data, but reports varied from, 'Occasional young shoots bitten off,' to 'Completely destroyed'. Quite a few recorded 'Totally untouched'.

Earlier in the book, I referred to my small, well screened netting cage, in which I grow a few roses for cutting. I also have runner beans, because they are so easy to grow, and I can pick them when they are young and tender. I grow sweet peas up the runner beans, and in spite of the failure predicted by the experts, they do extremely well. Occasionally, the pigeons will perch on the top bamboo canes and peck off a few of the sweet pea blooms, but as far as I can see never – or at least, far fewer of – the bean flowers. Home-made plastic cloches are used to get the plants past the very tender and vulnerable stage.

It will probably be obvious that the order of vegetable preference is not statistically accurate, because the commoner vegetables such as runner beans obviously attract more comments than, say, asparagus. But as a general guide I think that it gives a reasonable indication of the risk factor when deciding which vegetables to grow.

Fruit and Fruit Trees

Some contributors to the survey reported deer eating, say, apple or plum – without making it clear whether it was the fruit or the foliage, or both. In most cases it is both.

Apple.   Apples are irresistable to deer, who will stand on their hind legs to eat them, or to shake them down to the ground. They will take the flowers, buds, shoots and leaves also. Typical comments include: 'Six new apple trees chewed to the ground', 'Essential to wire in young trees' and 'Rigid Netlon has to be kept round my cordon apples and other cordon fruit'.

Crab apple (*Malus*).   For some reason, much less appealing than ordinary apples, though here and there leaves and shoots were eaten. One report stated that the crab apples were totally ignored, while the really common apples were taken – fruit and foliage. A lone fallow 'gorged on our yellow crab apples'.

Blackberry *(Rubus)*.   One or two garden varieties (such as 'Benenden', grown for its pure white flowers) were reported untouched, but the common bramble is a staple food in the wild – particularly of roe. The new, young growth is much favoured. According to the researcher Norma Chapman, there are different species of wild bramble: some are less palatable than others and are avoided. In California, their common bramble is resistant to white-tailed deer.

Blackcurrant.   Mostly resistant reports: only one 'eaten by roe', and in the author's garden one bush nibbled during a drought period though never previously.

Cherry.   Leaves, young shoots and fruit eaten, though two reports listed dessert cherries as *not* being eaten in high summer. One press report described deer chewing off the straps that kept the protective tubes in place, and then 'demolishing the newly planted saplings – one of their favourites'.

Currant.   (Flowering). The many reports on the strong smelling flowering, currant all say resistant, and the comments on the edible red and black currants agree. One case only of young blackcurrants being nibbled in drought.

Fig.   Mostly never touched, except for an occasional 'pruning' by red deer (Exmoor), but in the hotter climate of Portugal (also red deer) figs are vulnerable.

Gooseberry.   Relatively resistant. A number of 'not eaten' reports, (and from the USA – 'safe from white-tailed deer, but not from racoons!'). Some damage recorded, nevertheless. Mostly, leaves eaten – even from the thorniest varieties – and fruit mopped up when fallow broke into a fruit cage. In a pheasant covert wild gooseberries planted for the game resulted in 'not a leaf left and every top shoot eaten off in mid-July'. Apart from this one incident, bushes rarely badly damaged. Among the safer fruit to grow.

Medlar.   A single report: resistant.

Mulberry.   'No leaf or fruit remaining below about 4 ft (1.22 m) – single report on a dwarf, weeping variety.

Olives.   Eaten by fallow in Italy and red deer in Portugal, but said to be resistant to white-tailed deer in California. (Included only to record regional differences).

Peach.   A single report: '"Peregrine" never touched'.

Pear.   The vulnerability of the pear is reportedly less than that of some other favoured fruit. When damage occured, it was mostly to shoots and buds. One report said, 'Trees attacked, but fruit left' and another, 'Bush pears not touched by fallow'. Elsewhere, pears on the lower branches of espaliers were pulled off. Pears were included in general lists of fruit eaten, but not so often.

Plum.   A favourite: as with apples, deer will stand on their hind legs to reach them. One report said, 'Cherry trees and plums were attacked first – before other fruits. Leaves, shoots and fruit taken.' Another said: 'Our purple, Pershore plums were taken, but not a sharper, damson-like plum'. In another garden, the wild plum or bullace (*Prunus institia)* was untouched. The bark of plum trees suffered in some gardens.

Quince.   Several reports: resistant.

Raspberry.   Many reports of canes being damaged – particularly young ones: side shoots eaten, tops bitten off and so on. The fruit was 'Highly preferred'.

Rhubarb.   Resistant: One or two reports of odd leaves being torn off and partially eaten. (Leaves are poisonous to humans).

Strawberry.   Leaves mostly eaten in winter, the new shoots in the spring, and the fruit whenever available. One gardener wrote: 'Have given up growing them – a bed of ripening fruit cleared overnight'. Protection is essential. The local PYO nursery noticed damage to leaves and shoots, but said his fruit crop didn't appear to suffer – possibly because there was such a quantity on offer? One curious feature – some reports said 'Leaves only, not the fruit', while others said 'Fruit only, not the leaves'. The latter I can understand. In some gardens, *wild* strawberries were untouched.

Vines/grapes.   Damage occurs in some UK vineyards, but vines in three gardens not touched. No trouble reported in California, under heading 'Grapes', as opposed to 'Vines'.

Wild fruits. Deer enjoy acorns, beech mast, bilberries (and other vacciniums), chestnuts, rose hips, rowan berries and many other hedgerow offerings.

Trees

When researching material for this book, I decided not to include damage to trees, as the forestry authorities had covered the subject very thoroughly. However, several gardeners wrote in about their more ornamental trees such as **magnolias, tulip trees, catalpas, walnuts, golden yews** and the like, which would be of little interest to the commercial forester. As individual trees, unfamiliar to deer, they stood out and probably invited attention.

Correspondents also reported on some of the commoner forest trees, such as **Scots pine, ash, beech, chestnut** and so on, which are sometimes to be found in larger gardens. Because such trees would be growing singly or in small groups – or in the case of, say, **beech, *leylandii*** etc. as hedges – the reaction of deer to these trees in gardens was likely to be different to those in large, single-species plantations. For this reason, I am appending a brief note on the subject, distilled from about two hundred reports recieved from gardeners and foresters. The type of damage described was sometimes concerned with foliage or shoots that had been eaten, and at other times with fraying and barking. The difference was not always made clear. But whether a tree has been attacked by browsing or antler rubbing is probably not all that important to an enraged gardener! Furthermore, the age of the vulnerable trees was not always given, so the value of some of the information was to some extent lessened. As noted earlier, nearly all newly planted trees are at some risk, and should be protected for the first few years. Many will grow too tall and too tough in quite a short time, or lose their novelty interest, to be of much concern to the deer.

Magnolias, for example, were usually classed as resistant, but often qualified by an explanation that when they were very young a few shoots might be bitten off, in most cases causing minimal damage.

If the saplings are of the type that are best protected by plastic tubes – and the tender growth sprouting out of the top is constantly shaved off – the spiked collar should be used. Young **cherry trees** and **ash saplings** seem to have been particular favourites, but almost any fresh foliage poking out of a tube that is insufficiently high is at risk.

Conifers in general

Broadly speaking, conifers were reported as being less vulnerable than broad-leaved species. In fact, quite a few gardeners went so far as to state: 'Conifers are safe' or words to that effect. But it depends on the species: certainly some are less resistant than others. The untouched specimens were in the majority.

THE MORE RESISTANT SPECIES

One typical example said;- 'A **golden** *thuya plicata* (**western red cedar**) was never touched by either fallow or roe, but the conifer next to it was regularly shredded!' Unfortunately, the writer did not name the conifer that suffered. Another letter about *thuya* stated; 'This species is seemingly avoided by antelopes and zebras around my coffee and pawpaw crops in East Africa'. A New Forest ranger reported that *thuya* saplings were growing well in an area much frequented by fallow. Several mature *thuya* hedges were listed as never touched. I have one myself and am not surprised, but no reports were received of new plantings. Prudence suggests they should be protected until established.

Among other relatively trouble-free conifers which were mostly reported by commercial woodland owners, were: **Austrian Pine (*Pinus nigra*), Corsican Pine (*Pinus nigra var maritima*), Mountain Pine (*Pinus mugo*)** – new shoots eaten, but minimal damage. Most of the **Cypresses,** including **Leyland** (very minor damage). **Lawson** (dwarf variety **Ellwoodii,** slightly topped) and **Monterey (*macrocarpa*),** but a single *Chamaecyparis pisifera* **'Boulevard'** had been 'torn pieces on the ground'. (fraying?), **Italian cypress (*C. sempervirens*)** was also resistant. **Cedars, including the Japanese, the Blue and the Deodar. Larch (*Larix decidua*)** was rarely eaten, but suffered from bark stripping. One ten-year-old tree destroyed by roe. Regarding **Western Hemlock (*Tsuga heterophylla*),** a nearby area of natural regeneration is flourishing, so one presumes that hemlocks are not highly palatable.

VULNERABLE CONIFERS

Among the species most liable to attack by deer were: **Norway Spruce** (*Pinus sylvestris*) particularly when young and grown for the

Christmas tree market, young **Douglas fir** (*Pseudotsuga*): **Silver fir** (*Abies alba*): **Scots pine** (*Pinus sylvestris*): **Sitka spruce** (*Picea sitchensis*) and **Lodgepole pine** (*Pinus contorta*).

There were regional differences. Some of these reports were from gardeners, as well as timber growers.

Hardwoods

Rather as some gardeners stated: 'Conifers are safe!', others said: 'All deciduous trees are vulnerable – certainly in their early years – some more than others'. I would not disagree.

Ash (*Fraxinus excelsior*). The most vulnerable of all hardwoods: equally enjoyed by rabbits and grey squirrels.

Beech (*Fagus sylvatica*). Resistant except for browsing in hard weather: occasional bark-stripping, also undertaken by grey squirrels, which can cause serious damage. Possibly one reason why beech in plantations are left alone is that there is no real undergrowth to provide cover. This certainly applies to the shy roe, which would feel exposed. Fallow have different sensibilities. A local ranger told me that he saw a group of them lying down and watching very noisy forestry operations, involving a great deal of machinery, taking place nearby . They were not in the least concerned. In gardens, beech survive well.

Bird Cherry (*Prunus padus*). Usually ignored.

Elm (*Ulmus procera and spp*). Not many reports, probably because of Dutch elm disease problems. Some resistance noted, but one weeping elm cropped all round to nose height.

Gean or Wild Cherry (*Prunus avium*). Leaves sometimes browsed: some barking. Not high risk.

Hornbeam (*Carpinus betulus*). Vulnerable in the only two reports received.

Horse chestnut – Common (*Aesculus hippocastanum*). Mostly resistant.

Lime (*Tilia*). Even young trees resistant in a number of garden – but damaged (by fraying) in others, and in nurseries. At one time there were sizeable areas of small-leaved lime (*Tilia cordata*), in the New Forest, but as the deer numbers increased the limes were cropped to extinction. Self-generation was doomed to failure. A similar report was received from a forest in Kent. Must be classed as vulnerable.

Maple. Field (*Acer campestris*) **and Norway** (*Acer platanoides*).

Reports of young field maples actually killed, and Norway maple browsed. Hedge maples invariably recover from trimming. Ornamental garden maples, see under *Acer* in main list.

Oak English (*Quercus robur*) and Holm/Evergreen (*Quercus ilex*).   Acorns are a favourite food of deer, so the whereabouts of oaks would probably be routinely checked up on.

Pigs are equally acorn-minded. In Portugal, when the pigs are let loose in the oak plantations (as in the pannage months in the New Forest) they rush to their favourite acorn trees, remembering them from the season before. I doubt that deer are as discerning: but any acorn feast would attract them. On the Iberian peninsula the red deer damage both the evergreens and the cork oaks, and will rattle the branches vigorously to make the acorns fall to the ground!

Oak saplings are very vulnerable: a nearby area destined for natural regeneration was regularly eaten down to the ground until safely tubed. I was therefore surprised to read that in several gardens the English oaks (and one evergreen) were ignored. About the same number were attacked. In spite of the oaks growing safely in many gardens, they should be categorised as vulnerable.

Poplar (*Populus nigra* and *tremula*).   Some browsing and some bark-stripping reported. In Portugal it suffers from attacks by red deer.

Robinia (*Pseudoacacia*).   Few reports: side shoots browsed in one garden – tree survived. Another destroyed by barking (muntjac).

Rowan or Mountain Ash (*Sorbus aucuparia*).   The rowan must be a survivor. It is browsed in varying degrees and from time to time damaged by bark-stripping. The berries are much favoured by birds and beasts. Many of the rowans that were planted to keep the witches away from the old stone crofts in the Highlands, are still standing or at least their self-seeded descendants are, so obviously they have a degree of endurance.

To my surprise, a Surrey nursery – much frequented by roe, and growing several varieties of Rowan – has not suffered any casualties to its young potted-up saplings. In ordinary gardens more were reported as 'pretty resistant', than vulnerable.

My herb manual states that *aucuparia* means 'bird-catching' (Japanese, at a guess?): the berries being used by bird-catchers as baits in their traps. 'Rowan' itself is connected with 'rune' and could be called the magic tree. Clearly, no garden should be without one.

Silver Birch (*Betula spp*). Young birches tend to be vulnerable, and barking takes place at any age – particularly on the Paper birch. However, in just under half the gardens that reported on birch, deer caused no trouble. A weeping birch was among the untouched ones.

Southern Beech (*Nothofagus*). Resistant. (Single report).

Sweet Chestnut (*Castanea sativa*). Tree nursery reports 'Not normally browsed by roe', but some minor damage noted in parts of the New Forest.

Sycamore (*Acer pseudoplanatus*). Few reports from gardeners, but a favourite of a tame muntjac, which is probably not giving much away! (Possibly follows the same rather complicated categorising of other acers). Local foresters say that it is not a favourite of deer, but of grey squirrels.

Whitebeam (*Sorbus aria*). My neighbour showed me a young whitebeam (related to the Rowan), from which several shoots had been bitten off (by fallow) two seasons running. One other browsing casualty was reported.

Willow (*Salix* – various). Several reports on a variety of willows. 'Ignored' recorded more frequently than 'seriously damaged', which included 'munched by roe', '6 ft saplings badly barked by roe'. Risky not to protect when young.

Ornamental trees
The following were reported as 'resistant to deer' with no other details. The commoner name is placed first.

Catalpa (Indian bean tree) Mostly resistant, but lower leaves sometimes browsed.

Crape myrtle (*Lagerstroemia indica*)
***Ginkgo biloba* (Maidenhair tree)**
Gleditsia
***Halesia var vestita* (Silver bell, Snowdrop tree)**
Hoheria angustifolia
Katsura tree (*Cercidiphyllum japonicum*)
Persian ironwood (*Parrotia persica*). Needs protection when young: ignored when mature

Persimmon (*Diosphyros Kaki*)
Pistacia chinensis
Prunus 'Kursar'* and *'Pendula'
***Schinus* (Pepper-tree)**

Silk tree (*Albizia julibrissin*)
Sweet gum (*Liquidambar styraciflua*)
Tulip tree (*Liriodendron*)
Walnut, black (*Juglans nigra*) – 'tested, not eaten'

Chapter Twelve

Bites from Deer Ticks

Where deer are numerous, ticks are also likely to be present. A resident in the New Forest suggested that I should add a note on the subject, because in this area particularly, their bite can cause Lyme disease. This was only diagnosed in Britain in 1985: it is caused by a bacterium *Borrelia bungdorferi.*

Not all ticks carry the disease, but it is worth knowing some basic facts. My wife and I get bitten three or four times a year, so we are familiar with the problem. The ticks usually transfer to passers-by from long grasses, bracken etc. – mostly in the summertime. Even if one is wearing long trousers, as opposed to shorts, it is amazing where they fetch up!

Lyme disease normally – but not always – starts with a rash around the bite. This is accompanied – sometimes preceded – by flu-like symptoms, with aching joints and headaches, but some infected people have no symptoms at all. However, if such symptoms develop, see your doctor immediately; treatment with antibiotics is effective. If you delay, complications may develop.

If you feel an itchy sensation, do not scratch, but check (with a magnifying glass, if necessary) if a tick is biting you. They can be very small at this stage. Do NOT pull the tick off hastily and risk leaving the head in. As to dislodging the tick, I have seen it recommended that one uses the glowing end of a lighted cigarette to cause them to drop off. All I have ever succeeded in doing is burning myself!

If you are experienced and the tick is large enough, you may be able to twist it round gently until it comes away clean – using sharp finger nails or eyebrow pluckers to get a grip.

Alternatively, dab on meths, alcohol or nail varnish remover freely, until it falls off. Nail varnish – for hidden areas of the body – never fails. Put a thick blob on top of the tick and let it dry. Leave it there for about 48 hours, and then pick it off with a sharp finger-nail and sponge it off in the bath. The tick will be dead. The itching may continue for a few days after the tick has gone. Apply a little antiseptic.

An informative leaflet on Lyme disease is available from:- Dr E.P.Wright, Dept of Microbiology, Conquest Hospital, St Leonards-on-Sea, East Sussex, TN37 7RD. An SAE is required.

APPENDIX ONE

VULNERABLE OR RESISTANT?
Summaries of main plants.

These lists represent the observations of some three hundred gardeners who have helped with the survey. While this is only a small sample, I think it is fairly representative. If one takes into account the dozen or so horticultural clubs, garden societies, nurseries, official bodies and so on, who sent in a single list – summarising the reports of many members or customers – I think the size of the sample could easily be doubled.

The *highly vulnerable* category is likely to be the most straightforward and broadly correct. A gardener is almost certain to take instant notice if he finds a bed of tulips felled overnight, or a newly planted shrub gnawed down to its pristine label. But in the *resistant* lists there may be scores of lesser plants that have survived for years and are almost taken for granted. So this list, while not inaccurate, is included more for interest than guidance. It also shows the complexities of trying to put plants into rigid categories.

Inevitably, there are gaps in the lists because – as mentioned – uncommon plants are unlikely to have been included, and a number of very common ones may just have escaped notice, being judged too ordinary to bother about. For example, totally safe snowdrops should surely have been in the first half dozen of the resistant list and not featured in twenty-ninth place. Santolina – though ignored by deer – has very low points probably because it is not grown a great deal. Peonies placed at 20 are practically never touched, whereas poppies in third position are badly eaten in *some* gardens.

Obviously some confusion will arise when it is seen that the same plant is featured in both lists – resistant and otherwise. I have already discussed the problem of the plant that survives well in one garden, but is massacred in another, and I can understand the bafflement of a gardener who reads that, say, fuchsias are high on the resistant list,

109

when in his own garden they are mercilessly shredded. But here there is an explanation, of sorts. Much depends on the species of fuchsia. The hardy varieties – like the *magellanicas* – are rarely eaten, whereas the showy ornamental ones tend to be more appetising.

As to viburnums, it is also a question of the variety concerned. *V. opulus* is commonly eaten: *V. tinus* suffers three times as many eaten as ignored: and *V. fragrans (farreri)* is hardly ever touched. So like the fuchsias, viburnum – plain and simple – appears in both lists: eaten and ignored. If I had asked for comments on each of the fifty odd species listed in the *RHS Plant Finder*, the response might have been rather disappointing! With begonias there is a similar sort of explanation: in this case it is whether they are tuberous or fibrous-rooted. So they, too, can be classified as both vulnerable and fairly safe, according to their origin. The tuberous are more at risk.

Regarding azaleas, the evergreens suffer much more than the deciduous, though the latter do not escape entirely. Sedum appears on both lists, because *S. spectabile* is in most cases attacked by deer, while other sedum species are left alone. With a few plants, such as pelargoniums and some lilies – there seems to be no reasons why they are untouched in one garden and devoured in another, other than 'local conditions'. There are a number of such 'two-faced' plants. If only it was as simple as saying that all deer eat runner beans, or all woodpigeons eat acorns.

More detailed explanations are given under each plant name in the main lists that follow. These should be consulted when assessing the chances of new plants in a garden, and possible protective requirements.

Vegetables, fruit, herbs and a few selected 'garden trees' (such as Japanese maples, weeping willows, ornamental conifers etc.) commented on by correspondents have already been discussed in separate notes. One or two such as yew will be found in the summaries, because they are frequently mentioned. I am not quite clear as to the division between shrubs and trees. In many cases a shrub grows into a tree. The holly in our garden – at a height of twenty feet, – is certainly no longer a shrub.

Incidentally, some useful material regarding the habits and dietary preferences of white-tailed deer in gardens was received from professional nurseries and garden clubs in the USA. Some data was picked up on the Internet from States as far apart as Texas and Maryland. If the plants were listed in the RHS lists for the UK they

110

have been included. White-tailed deer are not dissimilar in their dietary preferences to our fallow.

Nomenclature
The plant names I have used will probably exasperate a botanist, but the way plants are classified by scientists can be confusing to the average gardener. Azaleas are rhododendrons and will not be found under 'A'. Michaelmas daisies are asters: Shasta and ox-eye daisies are members of the chrysanthemum family, as are marguerites. I have already mentioned 'geraniums', which are really cranesbills and not pelargoniums. A. G. L. Hellyer, the great writer on gardens of some forty years ago, put it so well when referring to the broom. 'The distinction between *genista* and *cytisus* is a purely botanical one. This is one of those instances where botany tends to confuse rather than clarify the issue so far as gardens are concerned'. In most cases I have used the names familiar to ordinary gardeners, but if you do not at first find what you want, try an alternative; in some cases I have listed both names.

Summary of Plants that are Most Resistant to Deer

(or more resistant than vulnerable)
listed in order of the number of reports received.

		Reports			Reports
1	Primula (inc hyb. primrose, polyanthus)	74	8	Sedum (with exception of *S. spectabile*)	52
2	Fuchsia (Mainly hardy varieties)	68		Lavender	52
3	Poppy (Some varieties not)	64	9	Elaeagnus (Some varieties)	51
4	Viburnum (Some varieties: inc. *V. burkwoodii, fragrans farreri.* See page 110)	63	10	Berberis	50
			11	Mahonia	45
5	Heathers	60		Rhododendron – excl azaleas. (See also vulnerable list)	45
6	Hydrangea	55			
7	Mallow (See additional list – vulnerable)	54	12	Iris	44
			13	Hosta	43

Reports   Reports

	Potentilla	43	25	Escallonia	25
	Brooms (inc *Cytisus, Genista*)	43	26	Azaleas (Mainly deciduous)	24
14	Cotoneaster	41		Geranium – evergreen. (cranesbill)	24
	Lilies – excl Hemerocallis. (See also vulnerable list)	41	27	Cistus	23
15	Pelargonium	38		Alchemilla (lady's mantle)	23
	Hypericum	38		Clematis	23
16	Buddleia	36		Pieris	23
	Euonymus (Often ignored, but not *reliably* safe)	36		Vincas	23
	Daffodil	36	28	Holly (Ilex)	22
17	Choisya	35		Philadelphus	22
18	Begonia (Mostly the bedding varieties)	34		'Laurel' (Prunus, Aucuba; excl Bay)	22
19	Hellebore	32	29	Snowdrop	21
20	Peony	31	30	Camellia	20
	Foxglove	31		Dogwood (Cornus)	20
21	Weigela	30		Senecio	20
22	Euphorbia	28	31	Skimmia	19
	Forsythia	28		Chaenomeles (Japonica)	19
23	Crocus (See note in introduction)	27	32	Aquilegia	18
	Jasmines	27	33	Artemesia (wormwood)	17
24	Daphne	26		Hebe	17
	Rosemary	26		Myosotis	17
	Spiraeas	26		Achillea	17
			34	Santolina	16
			32	Deutzia	14

Note: Very few reports on ferns received, but acknowledged to be very resistant – except a few varieties when very young.

Summary of the Main Plants that are Vulnerable to Deer

(or more vulnerable than resistant)
listed in order of number of reports received.

Reports

1 Rose — 87
2 Geranium – evergreen (cranesbill) (See additional list) — 70
3 Crocus (Presumed eaten by deer) * — 64
4 Pansy (Winter-flowering the most vulnerable) — 56
5 Tulip (See additional list) — 55
6 Pelargonium (See additional list) — 45
   Euonymus (Mixed reactions, but more vulnerable than resistant) — 45
   Viburnum (Some varieties: V. tinus the most vulnerable See Page 110 **) — 45
7 Fuchsia (Mainly hybrid, frost-tender varieties: others more resistant) — 44
8 Azalea (Mainly evergreen) — 39
9 Phlox (See additional list) — 38
10 'Laurels' (Inc Aucuba and Prunus varieties) — 34
11 Lilies (Other than Hemerocallis) — 33
   Sedum — 33
12 Camellia — 31
13 Hemerocallis — 29

Reports

   Hebe (Depending on variety: see additional list) — 29
   Primula (Inc hyb. primrose, polyanthus) — 29
14 Clematis — 28
15 Heathers (Mainly winter flowering) — 27
   Mallow — 27
   Yew (See additional list) — 27
16 Bluebell (See additional list) — 26
17 Ivy — 25
18 Begonia (Mostly tuberous) — 24
   Dianthus (carnations, pinks) — 24
   Hosta — 24
19 Honeysuckle — 22
20 Poppies (Many resistant: see main list) — 21
   Rhododendrons (Excl azaleas) (Mainly small-leaved varieties) — 21
21 Elaeagnus (Some varieties only) — 20
22 Bergenia — 19
23 Grape Hyacinth (See additional list) — 18
   Holly — 18

113

24 Philadelphus	17	29 Forsythia	10
Anemone (Japanese)	17	30 Hyacinth (See	
25 Cornus (dogwood)	16	additional list)	9
26 Lupin	14	31 Sweet pea (See	
Delphinium	14	additional list)	8
27 Wallflower (See		Michaelmas daisy	
additional list)	13	(*Aster novi-belgii*)	8
28 Sweet William (Dianthus)	11	Petunia	8

* See main lists for notes on other crocus eaters.
** See main lists for other varieties.

Extended List, with Some Additional Notes, on

PLANTS IN THE MOSTLY RESISTANT CATERGORY

A

Abelia (grandiflora – the best known). Occasionally in winter, but mostly safe.

Abeliophyllum. A. distichum. Resistant.

Abutilon. Most report safe, but one *new* plant eaten down.

Acacia (Mimosa). Resistant.

Acanthus (Bear's breeches). A number of resistant reports, but one *A. mollis* eaten.

Acer (Maple). Many varieties reported on.
Evidently, some species more vulnerable than others, i.e. Senkaki eaten regularly; *Aureum* and *Lutescens* to some extent; *Masukagami,* 'Bloodgood', *Shindeshojo, Chitoseyama,* and *Osakazuki* not eaten. Where no species mentioned, reports varied from 'much favoured' to 'ignored'.
More *Acers* undamaged than otherwise. (See also Trees for Field maple etc)

Achillea (Yarrow). Yellow and pink varieties very rarely eaten: white (The Pearl) occasionally cropped.

Aconite (Winter) *Eranthis hyemalis.* Resistant.

Aconitum (Monkshood). Resistant. (Very toxic: a dog died after chewing up a plant).

Actinidia (A.kolomikta) Twining climber. Resistant, but *A. kolomikta,deliciosa* and *polygama* can be shredded by joyful cats.

Agapanthus (African Lily). Only a single report of damage.

Agave. Resistant. (Single report).

Ageratum (Floss flower). Resistant.

Ajuga (Bugle). Resistant.

Akebia (Twining climber). *A. quinta.* Resistant.

Alchemilla (Lady's Mantle). Most reports say resistant, but a few record both deer and rabbit damage: 'Every flower is eaten'.

Allium. Related to onions, one would not expect trouble. In one garden a few stalks and buds bitten through, then spat out! Later, deer with eccentric palate actually ate a few.

Aloe. Resistant. (Single report).

Alstroemeria (Peruvian Lily). Mostly not eaten, but flowers occasionally stripped.

Alyssum. Resistant.

Amaryllis (Belladonna Lily). Resistant, but in one garden eaten down during drought.

Amelanchier (A. canadensis: Snowy Mespilus). Reports vary from 'untouched', (about half) to 'sampled', 'young shoots and flowers nibbled', and 'always fancied, needs netting protection'.

Amsonia (A. tabernaemontana). Resistant.

Anaphalis. Resistant.

Anchusa. Resistant.

Andromeda. Resistant. (Few reports).

Antirrhinum (Snapdragon). Not eaten in some gardens, but most record as vulnerable.

Aquilegia (Columbine). Resistant.

Arabis. Most reports say ignored, but (one report) badly cropped by sika.

Araucaria. A. araucana: (Monkey Puzzle.) Resistant.

Araujia (Cruel Plant). Resistant.

Arbutus (Strawberry Tree). *A. unedo.* Two reports of roe damage, and one (from Italy) of fallow eating. Otherwise resistant.

Arctostaphylos (Manzanita). Resistant.

Arctotis (African Daisy). Resistant. (Single report).

Armeria (A. maritima is thrift, sea pink: many other varieties). Resistant.

Aronia (Chokeberry). *A. arbutifolia.* Resistant. (Single report).

Artemesia (Wormwood). Resistant.

Arum (Lily). Wild *Arum* (cuckoo pint, lords-and-ladies) never eaten. Garden varieties mostly resistant.

Arum italicum 'pictum' resistant.

Arundo (decorative reed/grass). Resistant.

Asperula (A. odorata Sweet Woodruff*).* Resistant.

Astilbe. Most reports say resistant, but some recorded flowerheads bitten off and shoots nibbled: ie light damage.

Atriplex. Resistant. (Single report).

Aubretia. A single report of red deer eating, otherwise all resistant.

Aucuba. See Laurel.

Autumn Crocus See *Colchicum autumnale.*

Azaleas (Classified under the genus Rhododendron, but a distinct group). More reports of azaleas eaten than not, but many recorded no trouble at all – depending on varieties grown. In general, the *deciduous* varieties are mostly resistant – occasional young shoots and flower buds nibbled – whereas the small-leaved *evergreens* (Japanese) can be very attractive to deer, and need protection.

Azara A. microphylla. Resistant.

B

Ballota. B. acetabulosa. Resistant.

Balm – Lemon *(Melissa officinalis)* Resistant.

Balsam *(Impatiens balsamina).* Mostly resistant, but see related Busy Lizzie.

Bamboo *(Arundinaria).* Resistant.

116

Basil *(Ocimum basilicum)*. Resistant.

Bay *(Laurus nobilis)*. Resistant.

Beaucarnia recurvata (Elephant's foot, Pony-tail). Resistant. (Single report).

Berberis (Barberry). Mostly resistant: young plants occasionally destroyed, also a few cases of mature ones attacked.

Begonia.
Neither tuberous nor fibrous-rooted (bedding) eaten in many gardens, but in others both types may be eaten. *The tuberous being more at risk.* Rabbits will also eat.

Bergamot (Monarda. *M. didyma*, Bee Balm). Resistant.

Bergenia. Untouched in only a few gardens: class as vulnerable.

Betony *(Stachys officinalis)* Related to Lamb's tongues, Bunnies ears. Resistant.

Blackthorn *(Prunus spinosa* – Sloe). Resistant.

Borage *(Borago officinalis)*. Resistant.

Box *(Buxus)*. Resistant.

Broom *(Genista* and *Cytisus)*. Virtually resistant: a few reports of eating – many of fraying.
Spartium junceum. Spanish broom/ gorse. Resistant.

Brunnera *(B. macrophylla)*. Siberian bugloss, Perennial Forget-me-not. Resistant.

Buckthorn *(Hippophae rhamnoides* – Sea Buckthorn*)*. Resistant.

Buddleia (Butterfly Bush). Resistant: one *globosum* badly eaten. One *repens* nibbled. One young *davidii* 'topped', otherwise, largely ignored.

Bupleurum fruticosum (Shrubby hare's ear). Resistant. (Single report).

Busy Lizzie (*Impatiens:* Duet, Rosette, Novette, series etc). Reports about equal i.e. never touched – and eaten. Rabbits also eat, and one found in a tub of busy lizzies enjoying itself.

C

Calendula. See Marigold.

California poppy *(Eschscholtzia syn Romneya)*. Resistant.

Callicarpa. Resistant.

Callistemon (Bottle Brush). Resistant.

Calluna. See Heather.

Calycanthus (Californian allspice). Resistant. (Single report).

Camassia. Resistant.

Camellia. Fewer reported untouched than attacked, but letter asking for reports of damage in the RHS rhododendron/camellia journal drew not a single response. The older *japonicas* seem to be the least palatable. All varieties in author's garden badly trimmed by fallow January onwards. Ignored in summer – even new growth.

Campanula (Bellflower inc Canterbury Bell – *C. medium)*. Many varieties untouched; some more immune than others. Equally, in some gardens 'decimated'. Rabbits also eat. See vulnerable list for damage report. Some gardeners growing small species noted the *C. persicifolia, C. lactiflora* and *C. portenschlagiana* were untouched.

Candytuft *(Iberis). I. sempervirens* occasionally; otherwise annual and perennial mostly resistant.

Canna. Resistant.

Cardoon *(Cynala cardunculus)* Thistle-like. Resistant.

Carpenteria californica. Resistant. (Single report).

Caryopteris (C. clandonensis – Blue Spiraea). Resistant.

Cassia (Senna). Resistant. (Single report).

Ceanothus (Californian Lilac). Listed by various authorities and some individual gardeners as vulnerable, but on balance, slightly more resistant reports were received.

Cedar *(C. deodara* and others). Resistant.

Celandine *(Chelidonium).* Resistant.

Celosia cristata. Resistant. (Single report).

Centaurea. See Cornflower.

Centranthus (C. ruber – Red Valerian). Resistant. (Few reports).

Cephalaria. Resistant. (Single report).

Cerastium (Snow-in-summer). Resistant.

Ceratostigma (related to *Plumbago).* Resistant.

Chaenomeles (Japonica, Cydonia or Japanese quince). Resistant.

Chamaerops humilis (Fan palm) Resistant. (Single report).

Cherry *(Prunus).* Flowering cherries, such as 'Kanzan' or the prunus *subhirtilla autumnalis* usually ignored. (See under Trees for wild cherries).

Chicory *(Cichorium intybus).* Resistant. (Single report).

Chimonanthus (Wintersweet). Resistant, except for occasional winter nibble.

Chionodoxa (Glory of the Snow). Resistant.

Choisya (Mexican orange blossom). *C. ternata* highly resistant: occasional shoots nibbled, causing minimal damage.

Chrysalis *(C. francetii* Chinese Lantern). Resistant

Chrysanthemum.
(1) Florists or Japanese chrysanthemum (hyb. *C. morifolium).* Resistant with a few exceptions: mostly young plants – some pulled out of the ground, and 'Four rows of young plants destroyed'.
(2) *C. frutescens* or Marguerites. Resistant in some gardens, but vulnerable in others – equal proportions.
(3) *C. maximum.* Shasta, and moon or ox-eye daisies. Avoided in nearly all gardens, though eaten as 'second choice plant' by hungry fallow in Author's garden.

Cimicifuga (Bugbane). *C. racemosa* 'Only plant in woodland never touched'.

Cistus (Rock Rose). Most report resistant: an occasional 'nibbled', and a single 'destroyed by roe when covered in buds'.

Clarkia. See Godetia.

Clematis. Mixed reports: marginally more say 'side shoots nibbled', 'occasionally buds/flowers as well' and 'have to protect with Netlon' etc. than 'resistant'. No plants actually destroyed, and recovery usually fast. Herbaceous clematis often browsed, but also recovers.

Cleome (C. spinosa) Spiderflower. Resistant. (Single report).

Clethra (C. alnifolia Sweet pepper bush). Conflicting reports.

Colchicum autumnale (Autumn crocus; Meadow saffron). Resistant, except for a single report of a roe eating them in one garden.

Coleonema. C. pulchrum. Resistant. (Single report).

Comfrey *(Symphytum).* Mostly safe.

Coprosma. Resistant. C. *repens* and *C. kirkii.*

Cordyline (*C.* australis – New Zealand cabbage palm). Resistant.

Correa pulchella. Resistant. (Single report).

Coreopsis (C. tinctoria) Tick-seed. Resistant.

Cornflower *(Centaurea cyanum/montana* – annual and perennial). Fairly trouble-free: annual survives well in most gardens: perennial (*C. montana*) often grazed lightly, never killed. Only one report (variety not mentioned) says 'ravaged' (red deer and roe).

Cornus (Dogwood) Largely resistant, but a number reported 'eaten but recovered quickly', and 'needs protection' when young.

Corokia. (Wire netting bush). *C. cotoneaster.* Resistant.

Correa (C. pulchella). Resistant.

Corylopsis (Winter Hazel). *C. spicata* resistant in some gardens: elsewhere, other varieties regularly browsed.

Corylus (Hazel). Although hazel coppice is invariably heavily browsed in woodland, a number of correspondents reported that various hazels in their gardens were untouched, others, heavily attacked. Throwing back the brash on to the stool – once a favoured technique when coppicing – is now discouraged. It causes distorted, poor quality stems.

Cosmos. Mostly resistant.

Cotinus (C. coggygia syn Rhus cotinus: Smoke tree, Venetian sumach). Mostly resistant, but some reports of young growth eaten. Red-leaved variety particularly attacked.

Cotoneaster. Three times as many reported resistant as vulnerable. *Horizontalis* among the least eaten.

Cowslip *(Primula veris).* Most reported resistant, but a few recording damage asked, 'Could it be rabbits?'.

Crambe *(C. maritima:* Sea Kale). *C. cordifolia.* Resistant.

Cranesbills. See Geranium (evergreen, perennial).

Crataegus. See Hawthorn.

Crinodendron (Lantern tree). Mostly resistant, but one 'nibbled over many years – finally died'.

Crinum. Resistant. (Single report).

Crocus. Mixed reports – safe in a few gardens – but attacked in many more, particularly the yellow ones. (More details earlier in the book concerning crocus eaters – other than deer).

Currant (Flowering*: Ribes sanguineum)* Resistant.

Curry plant *(Helichrysum italicum).* Resistant. (Curry powder used as short-term deterrent).

Cyclamen (Hardy outdoor

varieties). Mostly resistant.

Cyntanthus. Resistant. (Single report).

Cyperus (inc bamboos, sedges etc). Resistant.

D

Daffodil *(Narcissus).* Untouched by deer in all but two UK reports. USA nursery observed flowers eaten (by white-tailed deer) during a severe food shortage.

Dahlia. Mostly avoided, but a few exceptions; 'Eaten down to stalks'; 'Dwarf dahlias in tubs early in season – later avoided'.

Daisy (Chrysanthemums). Most large daisies (inc shasta, ox-eye/moon) untouched in nearly all gardens. Eaten in only a few. Same applies to marguerites (*C. frutescens*).

Daphne. Many varieties: mostly resistant.

Datura (Angel's trumpets). Resistant.

Delphinium. Immune in some gardens, but on balance more reports of damage, varying from 'Tops nibbled' to 'Main stalks eaten right down'.

Desfontainia spinosa. Resistant.

Deutzia. Mostly resistant.

Dianthus (carnations, pinks etc). Sweet William *(D. barbatus)* under S. Untouched in some gardens: eaten in many more – usually buds and flowers.

Diascia. Resistant.

Dicentra (Bleeding Heart). More ignored than eaten: sometimes white eaten and red untouched.

Dichelostemma. D. *ida-maia* resistant. (Single report).

Dierama pulchermum (Wand Flower). Resistant. (Single report).

Diervilla *(Syn weigela).* Resistant. (Single report).

Diosma. Resistant. (Single report).

Dipelta. Resistant. (Single report).

Dodonaea. D. *viscosa:* resistant. (Single report).

Dogwood. See *Cornus.*

Doronicum (Leopard's Bane). Resistant . (Single report).

Dracaena (Dragon palm). Resistant.

Drimys (Winter's Bark). D. *winteri* resistant. (Single report).

E

Echinacea. E. *purpurea* resistant. (Single report).

Echinops (Globe Thistle). Resistant.

Echium (Annual Borage). The herb borage is usually safe, but *Echium* has been 'eaten when young'.

Elaeagnus (E. augustifolia) Oleaster. Many more resistant than otherwise. E. *pungens,* 'maculata' and 'Limelight' reported to be least palatable.

Elder *(Sambucus nigra).* Not really a garden shrub, but resistant.

Enkianthus (Pagoda bush). Usually resistant: one report of roe attack.

Epidemium. Varied reports. Flowers sometimes grazed off: often untouched.

Eremurus (Foxtail lily). Not eaten. (Single report).

Erigeron (Fleabane). Resistant. (Few reports).

Eryngium (Sea Holly). Mostly avoided, but E. *alpinum* and E. *planum* reported eaten.

Erysimum (Related to wallflower – *Cheiranthus*). Resistant.

Erythronium dens-canis (Dog's tooth violet). Resistant. (Single report).

Escallonia. New hedges sometimes difficult to establish, but apart from this, a great many more escallonias of different varieties were untouched than were eaten. At worst: 'Favourite winter food of roe'.

Eschscholtzia (Syn Romneya). See Californian poppy.

Eucalyptus. Never eaten (by red deer) in the plantations in Portugal, and mostly resistant in UK gardens, but young shoots (usually of *E. gunnii*) sometimes attacked. Also fraying damage and enjoyed by domestic goats!

Eucryphia. Mostly resistant.

Euonymus. Many reports. More were favoured as food items ('Chewed to the bone' . . . 'eaten to the ground' etc.) than escaped attention. The same varieties ('Emerald and Gold', 'Silver Queen', *E. europaeus* and others) were equally firmly put on the resistant list in some areas, as on the vulnerable list in others. One gardener puts *Euonymus* in her *very* worst category. The only policy can be to ask locally, proceed with caution, and certainly protect when young.

Eupatorium (E. purpureum) Joe Pye weed. Resistant. (Single report).

Euphorbia (Spurge). Resistant; only a single report of a wood spurge, *E. amygdaloides* eaten.

Euryops. Resistant. (Few reports).

Evening Primrose *(Oenothera)*. Occasionally ignored, but mostly eaten down.

Exochorda. *E. macrantha* (The Bride): single report 'not touched'.

F

Fatsia japonica (Castor oil plant). Divided opinions: both safe and vulnerable reports.

Ferns. Resistant, except for occasional young fern tips.

Feverfew *(Chrysanthemum parthenium)*. Resistant.

Fig *(Ficus)*. Normally resistant, but some minor damage reported by Exmoor hinds, and red deer will eat it in Portugal.

Filipendula (Meadowsweet). Resistant . (Single report).

Forsythia. Usually resistant, but side shoots sometimes nibbled, bark gnawed, and bushes subject to fraying. For some curious reason one lone bush in author's garden is almost spitefully eaten down annually, while other specimens are ignored except for gnawing/fraying.

Fothergilla. Resistant, apart from a single case of light damage (fallow).

Foxglove *(Digitalis)*. Resistant in gardens and in the wild, though eaten by tame muntjac confined in small trials area.

Freesia Resistant. (Single report).

Fremontodendron (Flannel flower). Resistant. (Few reports).

Fritillaria. *F. imperialis* (Crown Imperial), and another unnamed variety resistant (few reports).

Fruit. See separate chapter.

Fuchsia. Out of over one hundred reports, *more fuchsias were ignored than eaten.* These were largely the hardy ones like Magellanica, 'Riccartonii', 'Sharpitor', hardy Mrs Popple and the like. Magellicanicas with variegated leaves were eaten, and the new growth on any fuchsia was sometimes nibbled. While the hardy varieties were very occasionally eaten, it was mainly the large showy, frost-tender hybrids that suffered most – even shaved off in low, hanging baskets!

G

Gaillardia (Blanket flower). Ignored in some gardens: eaten in others. Slightly more resistant than otherwise.

Galium odoratum (Sweet woodruff). Resistant. (Single report).

Garrya elliptica. Mostly resistant: only one case of leaves stripped off.

Gaulthera shallon (Shallon). Mostly resistant, occasional browsing.

Gazania. Untouched in only a few gardens, see vulnerable list.

Gentian. Few reports: none recording damage.

Geranium (Cranesbill: perennial) Page 133 Pelargonium (Geranium) zonals, regals, ivy-leaved etc p 134

Geum (Avens). Equal resistant and vulnerable reports, but certainly 'at risk'.

Gladiolus. Resistant: only slight curiosity nibbling reported.

Globe thistle. See *Echinops.*

Grape Hyacinth. See *Muscari.*

Gunnera (G. manicata has prickly-edged leaves: about 5 ft (1.5 m) in height) Mostly avoided, but one *G. manicata* had some leaves eaten by roe.

Gypsophila. *G. elegans* survives, but *G. paniculata* (the florists' variety) heavily cropped.

H

Hamamelis (Witch hazel – *H. mollis,* the best known). Fairly resistant, but some fraying damage.

Hawthorn *(Crataegus)* Sometimes avoided: sometimes nibbled. Damage in gardens usually containable. Hampshire County Council put it in 'regularly browsed' category.

Hazel See *Corylus.*

Heathers *(Ericas* and *Callunas)* The different heathers have very varied palatability and nutrient content: but many more *(75%)* of the ornamental garden varieties were resistant, than were eaten. On the wild moorland, the animals (including deer) tend to avoid the *Ericas* and eat the *Callunas (C. vulgaris* or Ling being the main one) – which are more nutritious. But in gardens the winter-flowering varieties (*E. carnea*) which bloom Jan-April, are the ones that are attacked the most, though plenty are left unscathed. Some sika in Dorset actually pulled away the protective netting to get at the plants. *Erica cinerea* (summer flowering bell heather) has also been eaten when in bloom, while the nearby nutritious *Calluna* was left untouched. Experts suggest that the winter-flowering heathers are not necessarily preferred because food can be short at this time of the year, but because they are more palatable. Are deer, for example, attracted to the nectar? A number of gardeners reported that some judicious grazing improved the quality of their plants. Rabbits also eat heather. Tree heathers (*E. arborea*) tend to be avoided.

Hebe. More vulnerable than otherwise: nevertheless many varieties untouched. See additional vulnerable list.

Helenium. H. autumnale resistant . (Single report).

Helianthemum (Rock rose, sun rose). Only slight grazing reported, but also eaten by rabbits.

Helianthus (Sunflower). Mostly resistant, but small-bloomed variety topped at 2 ft (60 cm) high by fallow – two years running – in author's garden.

Helichrysums. Many varieties often used in patio containers, hanging baskets etc (plain, silver-grey or variegated). *H. petiolare, H. bracteatum* for drying, the Curry plant and others. Resistant.

Hellebore (Christmas rose, Lenten rose). Resistant. The wild ones in the Austrian mountains never touched by the local deer: allegedly toxic. Minimal damage in the UK.

Hemerocallis (Daylily). Here and there untouched, but must be classified as vulnerable.

Hesperis (H. matronalis) Sweet rocket. Resistant. (Single report).

Heuchera (Coral flower). More reported untouched than eaten.

Hibiscus (Tree hollyhock). Largely resistant.

Holly *(Ilex).* Although untouched in the majority of gardens, holly is regularly eaten in some, and must be classed as vulnerable. In the New Forest, it used to be cut down by the keepers and fed to the deer as winter browse: it was, in fact, known as 'browse-wood' and preferred when slightly wilted. Variegated plants seem to be the most vulnerable. Young holly plants should be protected.

Hollyhock. A 'second choice' plant – not entirely safe though avoided in many gardens.

Honesty *(Lunaria).* Usually avoided, apart from one 'heavily browsed in small garden, where tame muntjac were confined'.

Honeysuckle *(Lonicera)* Woodbine. Flowers, leaves and side shoots within reach are often eaten, but the damage is not usually severe enough to kill off a plant. Comments varied from 'occasional nibbling' to 'eaten avidly by sika'. Almost as many reports said 'ignored'. 'Fairly resistant' would be an accurate description. *Lonicera nitida*, the evergreen, small-leaved, hedging variety never touched.

Hops *(Humulus).* Hop growers report 'no problem'. (Rabbits cause major damage), but all bottom leaves of a hop plant eaten in author's garden by fallow during very dry seasons.

Hostas. Twice the number of reports stated 'not touched' compared with 'eaten'. There were also several variations on, 'The snails ate them all before the deer found them'!

Houttuynia (a marginal water plant). Resistant.

Hyacinth. See vulnerable list: not entirely safe. Blooms not eaten, if they survive to that stage.

Hydrangeas. Only a few reports of damage – mostly when young. Safer to protect at this stage.

Hypericum (St John's wort). Resistant.

I

Iberis. See Candytuft.

Impatiens. See Busy Lizzy.

Incarvillea. Resistant. (Single report).

Ipheion. Resistant. (Few reports).

Iris (Many varieties – both bulbous and rhizomatous) Mostly untouched, ('Flags' the most resistant). *Young* bearded irises and the more slender delicate irises are sometimes eaten or the heads are ripped off, but on the whole they are not liked by deer.

Itea ilicifolia. Resistant. (Single report).

Ivy. Must be classified as vulnerable, though untouched in a number of gardens. A regular winter food of deer in the wild.

Ixia (the Corn lily of South Africa). Resistant. (Single report).

J

Jasmine (Summer and Winter: not usually separated in reports). Both types overwhelmingly reported as resistant. Only one 'occasionally nibbled by roe'.

Juniper (Many varieties). Predominantly resistant in gardens, though in the wild, sometimes eaten in hard winters.

K

Kalmia latifolia (Calico bush). Reported 'untouched' and 'eaten' in equal numbers. In one garden the muntjac ate the *kalmia*, but the fallow did not.

Kerria. *K. japonica.* Resistant.

Kniphofia (Red-hot poker). Resistant – many reports: only one dissenting voice – 'Decimated by roe and muntjac'.

Kochia scoparia (Burning bush). Resistant. (Single report).

Kolkwitzia. Resistant.

L

Laburnum. Mainly resistant: one case of some suckers being eaten. (Supposedly toxic?).

Lamium (Dead nettle – many varieties). Mostly resistant; probably because available as a prolific 'carpet'. A single report of a roe 'greedily nibbling away' at *galeobdolon variegatum* end-March.

Lantana. Resistant. (Few reports).

Larkspur *(Consolida).* Resistant. (Single report).

Laurels (including *Prunus, Laurocerasus* and *Aucuba japonica*) Many divergent reports – views equal. Damage worst in winter. All exposed New Forest garden hedges are regularly kept trimmed by the free-ranging cattle as though cut with shears. Where the deer have got used to eating laurel, 'They will push wire netting aside to get at it' and, 'Even Portugal laurel, which we were assured was deer-proof, is eaten!'. However, as stated, there were equally as many reports of total disinterest in laurel.

Lavatera. See Mallow.

Lavender Resistant, though one captive muntjac was observed eating lavender. The stems can be very brittle and many report smashed plants as a result of trampling.

Lemon Balm (*Melissa*). Resistant.

Leptospermum. Resistant.

Leucojum (Summer snowflake). Resistant. One report of buds disappearing – culprit unidentified.

Leucothoe. Inconclusive reports, but certainly untouched in some gardens.

Leycesteria formosa (Himalayan honeysuckle, Pheasant Berry). Mostly resistant, occasional minor damge, or 'flowers only'.

Libertia. Resistant. (Single report).

Ligularia. Resistant. (Few reports).

Lilac *(Syringa).* Largely resistant: lower leaves occasionally browsed.

Lilies (excluding *Hemerocallis*). A great many reports – more resistant than otherwise, but many different lilies eaten in many gardens. Young growth from recently planted lilies the most susceptible.

Hybrid lilies – often the buds – sometimes sampled and then spat out, but others eaten down. Hybrids are probably not a 'first choice' food item and often escape entirely. When planted in groups of four or five, one or two may be eaten, but rarely the whole lot.

Less trouble with Martagons (the Turk's cap), which are never eaten in the wild. *L. regale* and *L.*

candidum untouched in many gardens: Arums do not escape entirely and should be routinely protected where susceptible. (Their wild counterpart cuckoo pint or lords-and-ladies never touched). *L. amaryllis* Belladonas survived untouched in the Author's garden for four seasons until a drought year, when they were all eaten down. The following year they recovered and flowered prolifically, as usual. Rabbits will eat lilies, and badgers dig up the bulbs.

Lily of the valley *(Convallaria).* Resistant: never eaten by the wild deer in the Austrian mountains. In UK gardens, an 'all clear' except for one 'occasional nibbling', and one 'flowers only'.

Limnanthese (Poached egg flower). Mostly resistant reports, but one, 'Avidly by sika'.

Limonium. See Sea Lavender.

Linaria (Toadflax). Resistant. (Few reports).

Liriope (LilyTurf). Resistant. (Few reports).

Lithospermum. Mostly resistant – an occasional nibble reported.

Lobelia. Reports equal on resistant or otherwise. *L. cardinalis* marginally suffering the most.

London Pride *(Saxifrage x urbium).* Mostly resistant, though a few crowns were eaten out in one garden by fallow (or rabbits?). One report of roe damage – 'only stalks left'. *S. fortunei* and other varieties of *Saxifrage* uneaten.

Lonicera nitida (Evergreen, including 'Baggesen's Gold'). See Honeysuckle.

Lotus (L. berthelotti 'Coral fan' or

'Parrots Beak'). Resistant. (Single report).

Lovage *(Levisticum officinale)*. Resistant.

Lunaria. See Honesty

Lupins. Variable reports. As 'sweet lupins' are planted as high protein stock feed on some of the less fertile soils, I would have assumed that lupins were palatable. Half the reports state 'not eaten', but the others report: 'some damage'; 'eaten a bit'; 'attacked once' etc.; one 'with relish!'. (The author's tree lupins eaten down till early summer, then ignored). A curious report stated '*yellow* picked out from a clump of *mixed* colours'.

Lychnis (Campion). Mostly resistant: a single report of flowers and leaves eaten by roe.

Lysichiton (inc two varieties of water/bog plants). Resistant. (Few reports).

Lysimachia (Loosestrife). Mostly resistant.

M

Macleaya (Plume poppy). Resistant.

Magnolia. Resistant, except for minor fraying damage, occasional nibbling of young shoots. Protect when young.

Mahonia (M. aquifolium, M. japonica and others). Resistant: a few reports of flowers eaten and tender spring shoots.

Malus. See Crab apple.

Malva (Mallow). Mostly resistant.

Marguerite *(Chrysanthemum frutescens)*. Rarely a favourite choice, but sometimes eaten.

Marigold *(Tagetes)* African and French, English *(Calendula)*. Marginally more were reported resistant than eaten. In spite of the pungent smell, some plants were eaten down to the ground. Regarding the pot marigold or calendula, there was little difference.

Marsh marigolds *(Caltha palustris)* – see additional vulnerable list.

Marvel of Peru *(Mirabilis jalapa)* Four o'clock flower. Some resistant reports, but not totally safe – probably a 'second choice' plant.

Meadowsweet *(Filipendula)*. Inconclusive reports: sometimes ignored.

Meconopsis (Himalayan Blue poppy and Welsh poppy). Resistant.

Melaleuca *(A. myrtle)*. Resistant. (Single report).

Melianthus (M. major: Honey bush). Resistant. (Single report).

Melissa. See Balm – lemon.

Mesembryanthemum (M. criniflorum) Livingstone Daisy. Reports varied.

Michaelmas daisy *(Aster novi-belgii)*. Many more 'never touched' reports than otherwise, but where damage occurs it can be severe.

Mignonette (Reseda) R. odorata. Resistant. (Few reports).

Mimulus. Mostly resistant. Pulled out of containers and abandoned in author's garden: a few nibbled.

Montbretia *(Crocosmia)*. Mostly resistant.

Morning Glory *(Ipomea)*. Resistant. (Single report).

Mountain Ash *(Sorbus)* Rowan. See Tree list.

126

Muscari (Grape hyacinth). Avoided in some gardens, but leaves often eaten, less so blooms. (Voles also eat). On the whole vulnerable.

Myoporum. Resistant. (Single report).

Myosotis (Forget-me-not). Mostly resistant.

Myrtle *(Myrtus).* Mostly resistant: only one young myrtle reported attacked, and some damage recorded by fallow in Italy.

N

Narcissus. See Daffodil.

Nasturtium (Tropaeolum). More resistant reports than not, but among the 'favoured' comments: 'flowers only', 'Flowers and stalks, not leaves', and 'Deer love them' (both roe and fallow).

Neillia (N. thibetica – the most common). One resistant, and one 'Young growth stripped off'.

Nemesia. Resistant. (Single report).

Nepeta (Catmint). Resistant: only one dissenting voice, (but cats will shred and eat large quantities of the plant).

Nerine. Most report resistant: one 'sampled'.

Nicotiana (Tobacco). More report resistant than not. *N. sylvestris* (the branching variety) never touched. Among the damage reports – 'Low blooms pulled off and left', 'Leaf tips only' – but one 'White tobacco eaten down'.

Nierembergia. Resistant. (Single report).

Nigella. (N. damascena. Love-in-a-mist). Resistant. Only one report 'grazed in drought'.

O

Oleander (Nerium oleander). Resistant. (Few reports).

Olearia (Daisy bush). Mostly resistant: one *O. macrodonta* eaten by muntjac.

Omphalodes. O. cappadocica resistant. (Single report).

Ophiopogon (O. japonicus). Resistant also to rabbits. (Single report).

Origanum. (*O. vulgare* 'Aureum' often planted: related to marjoram and used as a culinary herb, as well as a border plant. Resistant.

Osmanthus (usually *O. delavayi* or *O. burkwoodii,* Fragrant Olive). Mostly very resistant, but one 'Avidly eaten by sika', and one 'Eaten in winter'.

Osmunda regalis (Royal fern). Resistant.

Osteospermum. Resistant.

Ozothamnus. Resistant. (Single report).

P

Pachysandra. Resistant.

Palms. A number of varieties reported as resistant.

Pampas grass *(Cortaderia selloana).* Mostly untouched, except for fraying. Also some young plants damaged, young shoots eaten and one 'Pulled to pieces when plumes are in full glory'!

Passion Flower *(Passiflora).* Resistant. (Single report).

Penstemon. Mostly resistant.

Peony. Resistant. (Tree peony sometimes lightly browsed).

Pernettya (Prickly Heath). Resistant.

Perovskia (P. atriplicifolia Blue Spire'). Resistant.

Petunia. Mixed reports, but marginally more resistant than vulnerable. Probably a 'second choice' food item. Planted in garden tubs in two gardens and untouched until August. Elsewhere, intermittent damage.

Philadelphus (Mock orange). Marginally more totally resistant reports than eaten. Among the sufferers, many reported young plants being nibbled or occasionally browsed: new growth eaten within reach etc. Stressed the need for protection when young.

Phlomis (P. fruticosa, Jerusalem Sage and other varieties). Resistant.

Phlox. Avoided in only a few gardens: see vulnerable list. The mound forming *P. subulata* and *P. douglasii* less palatable.

Phormium tenax (New Zealand flax). Resistant.

Photinia (P. fraseri 'Red Robin'). Untouched in half the reports, in the others – 'red shoots always eaten'.

Phygelius. P. capensis resistant. (Single report).

Physocarpus. 'Dart's Gold' resistant. (Single report).

Pieris. Untouched in many more gardens, than damaged. New shoots sometimes nibbled. In two gardens, the blooms pulled off 'Debutante' and left on the ground. *P. japonica* and *P. formosa var forestii* said to be among the most vulnerable.

Plumbago. P. capensis. Resistant (Single report).

Pointsettia *(Euphorbia pulcherrima).* Resistant. (Single report).

Polemonium (Jacob's ladder). More resistant than eaten reports.

Polygonum (P. bistorta 'Superbum', and other varieties). Marginally more avoided than eaten. In the latter category, one 'Flowers eaten: later plants wrecked'. (roe): others 'Lightly browsed, but recovered completely'.

Poppy *(Papaver)* Excluding *meconopsis* and Californian poppy). One of the most controversial flowers, *but three times as many completely avoided as eaten.* (Rabbits will eat certain varieties, including Shirleys). One problem in assessing the vulnerability concerns the difference between, say, slight and slender Shirley poppies or opium poppies, and the sturdy , hardy orientals. Not all reports stated which variety, but I could not detect a great deal of difference among the varieties that were named.

Probably Shirley would be the commonest poppy in gardens, in which case it scores top for being ignored. Iceland (*nudicale*) and Opium, (*somniferum*) were about equal, also the orientals. In this latter group the buds suffered greatly. One writer said 'Eaten to extinction'. Many singled out Perry's White as being particularly vulnerable, others said 'Any white oriental and Perry's white, but not the nearby orange and pink' (muntjac).

One poppy grower mentioned that her Sultan's *P. paeoniaeflorum* 'did not attract the same edible interest. Did the deer think they were actually peonies (which they never eat)?' This lady used her hum-line successfully to deter her poppy eaters. An observer told me how he watched a roe going into a cereal crop and pick off the scarlet wild poppy heads.

Potentilla. Very resistant: a single case of roe eating flowers of 'Miss Willmot'.

Primula (inc Primroses and Polyanthus). Cowslip – *Primula veris* – under C. Oxlip – *Primula elatior* – under O in additional vulnerable list. Wild primroses are practically never eaten – a single record of muntjac eating.

Many reports on cultivated varieties, and all members of the primula family were largely resistant. Twice as many gardens reported no problems with primulas or polyanthus, as those that suffered damage. But where deer were eating them, the damage could be severe. These reports varied from 'sometimes' to 'avidly'. 'Polyanthus flowers stripped in early spring' was often recorded. On some occasions *newly planted,* brightly coloured hybrid primroses were pulled out of containers. Some left on the ground untouched, others had the centres eaten out. After replanting, they tended to be left alone. Probably curiosity.

Some species of bog-side primulas 'Vanished – roots and all – presumed carried off by the muntjac. Trouble stopped when wire netting was placed over remaining plants'.

To plant in large groups gave some protection, and solace.

Many correspondents suspected rabbit damage, but no evidence offered.

Privet *(Ligustrum).* Basically a survivor, but any isolated golden privet tends to be nibbled in some gardens.

Prostanthera (Mint bush). *P. cuneata* resistant. (Single report).

Prunella vulgaris (Self-heal). Resistant. (Single report).

Prunus. See Trees for small ornamentals.

Pulmonaria (Lungwort). Mostly flowers eaten, but one 'cropped to the ground' (sika). *P. saccharata, P. officinalis,* 'Sissinghurst White', survivors in some gardens, but see also vulnerable list.

Pyracantha (Firethorn). Mostly resistant, but in spite of sharp thorns, one report of 'a young hedge eaten up to nose height by determined roe'; 'young leaves stripped in spring', and one 'occasionally by sika'.

R

Red-hot-poker. See *kniphofia.*

Rhododendron. The larger leaved varieties are normally resistant, except in very hard weather. The local Forest keepers used to cut rhododendron leaves (presumably *ponticum*) as winter browse. However, the smaller-leaved species are attacked – mainly the buds and young shoots, and there were a few reports of the flowers being eaten.

A specialist grower in Scotland wrote: 'None are entirely safe, even a large-leaved rhodo was demolished (by roe) before we started enclosing areas with netting'. But another grower in Surrey (also invaded by roe) experienced minimal trouble, as does the author in his 'hungry' garden frequented by fallow.

One gardener asserted that certain varieties were habitually ignored,. but others – for example, young *quinquefolium* – leaves, were always eaten: as was *R. grande* (and a number of others). Another report also suggested that deer were selective in their choice of which ones to eat: a further report noted that certain buds were definitely preferred to those of other species.

On balance, from some seventy reports, nearly *three quarters recorded no or little damage* – except for occasional fraying, and the trampling of young plants.

Rhus *(Sumach).* Mostly resistant – only occasional nibbling.

Ribes (R. sanguineum) Flowering currant. Resistant: a single case of eating, and some 'bark rubbing'.

Robinia pseudoacacia. Mainly resistant: one three-year-old tree destroyed by 'barking'. (See also under Trees).

Rodgersia (R. aesculifolia) Resistant. (Few reports).

Romneya. See California poppy.

Roses. See chapter 12.

Rowan. See Trees.

Rudbeckia (Coneflower). Resistant: one 'rarely'.

Russian Vine *(Polygonum baldschuanicum).* Resistant.

S

Salvia (excluding the herb Sage). Mostly resistant.

Santolina (S. chamaecyparissus), Cotton Lavender. Resistant.

Saponaria (Soapwort – so named because it was planted near wool mills in olden times, and used in the washing of wool). Opinions equally divided regarding vulnerability.

Sarcocca (Sweet Box). Resistant.

Satureja (S. montana Winter savory). Resistant. (Single report).

Saxifrage (S. urbium London Pride). Resistant: also *S. fortunei.*

Scabious. Mostly resistant, but some reports of roe eating.

Schizostylis (Kaffir Lily). Mostly resistant.

Sea Buckthorn *(Hippophae rhamnoides).* Resistant.

Sea Lavender *(Limonium).* Resistant. (Few reports).

Sedum (Stonecrop). Many conflicting reports, but in total *more reported resistant than eaten.* Regarding the two commonest varieties, more *S. spectabile* (Ice plant) were eaten than avoided, and conversely more 'Autumn Joy' were spared than were eaten. Some of the *spectabile* sedums were 'chewed down when young': 'only nibbled', or 'nibbled in frosty weather'. In spite of these comments and the fact that more were resistant than not, sedums cannot be classed as other than 'at risk' according to variety.

Sempervivum (Houseleek). Mostly resistant, but one report of *S. tectorum* (the common houseleek) being eaten.

Senecio (S. maritima, laxifolius and

greyi among the best known). Mostly resistant.

Sidalcea. Slightly more resistant reports, than vulnerable.

Silene (Campion). Resistant.

Sisyrinchium (Pigroot). Resistant.

Skimmia. Resistant.

Snowberry *(Symphoricarpos).* On balance resistant, but one gardener has to protect young plants.

Snowdrop. Resistant.

Solidago (Golden rod). Mostly resistant: some reports of 'slight nibbling', 'topped this year for first time' etc. In author's garden, however, it is regularly enjoyed by fallow.

Solomon's Seal *(Polygonatum x hybridum).* Mostly resistant: sawfly larvae often remove all foliage.

Sorbaria. Resistant.

Sorbus (Rowan). See Trees.

Spiraea. Resistant.

Stachys (S. lanata – Lamb's ears: also 'Silver Carpet'). Resistant.

Stocks. Conflicting reports.

Stranvaesia. Marginally more resistant than otherwise. Arboretum reports 'badly barked'.

Stuartia (S. pseudocamellia and others). Resistant. (Few reports).

Styrax (S. japonicus). Resistant. (Few reports).

Sunflower. (See *Helianthus*).

T

Tagetes. See Marigold.

Tamarisk. Resistant.

Teasel *(Dipsacus).* Resistant.

Thalictium (Meadow Rue). Resistant.

Thrift or Sea Pink. See *Armeria.*

Tobacco. See Nicotiana.

Tolmiea. Resistant.

Tradescantia (Spiderwort). Mostly resistant; one report of blue-flowered variety being eaten.

V

Valerian *(Valeriana officinalis).* Resistant: but variety Phu 'Aurea' wiped out (single report). Also Red Valerian *(centranthus)* flowers eaten (single report). Attracts cats.

Veratrum (False hellebore). Resistant. (Single report).

Verbascum (Mullein). Resistant.

Verbena. Marginally more resistant than otherwise: flowers sometimes pulled off.

Veronica (Speedwell). Resistant.

Viburnum. See page 110. In general, about two thirds of all *viburnums* mentioned are more resistant than vulnerable. Most of these tend to be the deciduous varieties.

Vinca (Periwinkle). Resistant: some cropping of *V. minor* in hard weather.

Violet *(Viola).* Wild violets largely left alone, but garden varieties such as *V. odorata* vulnerable – see other list. The wild pansy (Heartsease) sometimes escapes attention (one very positive report from a deer-ridden garden) but not always.

W

Wallflower. See additional vulnerable list.

Weigela. Largely resistant, though some damage reported- especially to variegated plants.

Winter Aconite. See Aconite.

Wisteria. Mature shrubs resistant: some damage reported to young plants: 'Flower trusses neatly removed'.

Y

Yucca *(Y. filamentosa).* Resistant.

Z

Zantedeschia (C. aethiopica). Resistant. (Few reports).

Zinnia. One report, 'Eaten down by roe', but two others, 'Completely safe', and some resistant reports from USA.

Some Additional Vulnerable Plants (with Informative Notes)

Anemone (A. coronaria, de Caen, St Brigid etc). Sometimes eaten at flowering time. (Few reports).

Antirrhinum (Snapdragon). Not touched in a number of gardens, but must record it as vulnerable.

Aruncus (Goat's beard). Mostly vulnerable.

Aster *(Callistephus:* China or annual Aster). Vulnerable.

Azalea. See in Resistant List some information regarding vulnerable species.

Bluebell *(Hyacinthoides).* Very palatable to deer, who will eat down the new spring growth to within two or three inches of the ground. This usually grows up again – though a little weaker – and very often flowers. The blooms are mostly left untouched, but not always. The Forestry Commission reported that bluebells were in danger of being almost totally destroyed in some areas where the muntjac had undergone a population explosion.

Convolvulus cneorum. Vulnerable.

Geranium (Perennial evergreen, Cranesbills.) Vulnerable – frequently eaten down regularly. Typical comment, 'Our roe can't leave 'em alone'. Sometimes just the flowers are cropped, and there are a minority of gardens where they are ignored. There is some evidence that they prefer the blue varieties such as 'Johnsons's Blue' to the pink ones like 'Wargrave'.

Godetia (syn Clarkia). More eaten than not.

Grape hyacinth *(Muscari).* Very palatable to deer, but sometimes a few flowers manage to escape the early season cropping. They are also trimmed by voles.

Griselinia littoralis. Very vulnerable.

Hebe (Herbaceous varieties sometimes called Veronica) There are about 300 varieties of *Hebe,* comprising some very different plants. This is probably why half of the reports state 'severe damage', 'always fancied' and 'eaten all year round',and the other half say firmly 'not touched'. It must largely depend upon which variety is on offer. In one garden, for example, a group of Bowles's hybrid was untouched, but others nearby were all eaten down.

Hyacinth. Being a domesticated version of the bluebell, it is not surprising that deer will eat them. They are usually attacked when they have three to four inches of growth above the ground. If some escape attention and grow to their full height, their blooms are usually ignored. In some gardens hyacinths seem to be resistant. Several letters suggested that the pink ones were eaten, while the blue ones mostly escaped attention. (The opposite to cranesbills – probably coincidence).

Mallow Although resistant reports heavily outnumber eaten ones, if local deer take to shrub mallows – as in the author's garden – they will be relentlessly savaged.

Marsh Marigold *(Caltha palustris)*. Reports varied from 'Some years young shoots and leaves taken – other years not', to 'The muntjac wade in to decapitate them'.

Oxlip *(Primula elatior)*. A report of fallow taking flowers and leaves over a long period, and causing wholesale destruction in a certain area. Birds and rabbits will take a few flowers, but do no serious damage.

Pelargonium (Bedding geraniums, Regals, ivy-leaved etc). On

balance, a few more reported eaten than not: often only the flowers, and rarely the varieties with aromatic leaves.

Phlox (Annual, perennial and dwarf). The perennials are overwhelmingly vulnerable to deer, though a few gardeners with high deer numbers said theirs were untouched. Some of the dwarf varieties (*P. subulata*) were among the resistant ones. Very few reports on the annual (*P. drummondii*). One correspondent finds that leaving the dry stems standing from the previous year has some deterrent effect.

Pittosporum (P. tenuifolium the most popular). Avoided in a few gardens: browsed in slightly more.

Pulmonaria (Lungwort). Marginally more vulnerable reports than otherwise: mostly the flowers eaten, but one 'cropped to the ground'. *P. officinalis, P. saccharata* and one of the white varieties were among the more resistant varieties.

Ranunculus. Vulnerable.

Scilla. Eaten down like bluebells.

Sweet pea *(Lathyrus).* Mostly vulnerable, though many other pests eat sweet peas, from the buried seed to the tender young plants, and (woodpigeons) the flowers at a height of 6 ft (1.8 m) or more. Probably to some extent 'second choice' plants as comments were made such as: 'Sweet peas are strangely safe'; 'A single roe who nipped a few plants at the bud stage appeared not to like them'; 'Sampled, but did not persevere', and so on.

134

Sweet William *(Dianthus)*. More vulnerable than resistant, but never touched in some gardens and eaten intermittently in others. e.g. 'They by-passed my Sweet Williams last year and gave me a great show!'

Tulip. Frequently beheaded with relish – blooms, buds and stalks. (See main text concerning single roe who ate one hundred in one night). One correspondent reported that he planted daffodils and tulips together in one tub, and only the tulips were taken. Others said that two or three varieties had been avoided (but did not say whether this happened every year). For this reason – and that it may just have been chance – I hesitate to list them.

Badgers will dig up the bulbs.

Wallflower *(Cheiranthus)*. Twice the number of vulnerable than resistant reports, but certainly ignored in several gardens. Damage occurs mostly when newly-planted and also during hard weather. It seems to cease at, or just before, the buds break. Probably a 'second choice' plant, as some reports say: 'Occasionally damaged', 'Eaten for the first time this season'. Rabbits will also eat – mostly, in hard weather.

Water lily *(Nymphaea)*. Vulnerable: 'Roe will stand eating my water lilies, while I watch . . .' and 'I have seen muntjac wading in to eat white water lilies'.

Yew *(Taxus)*. A very palatable browse – particularly the new shoots. Highly vulnerable. The *fresh* foliage is not toxic to deer. According to Arthur Cadman, a retired Deputy Surveyor of the New Forest, 'Yew is much eaten in the Forest, where it was planted widely in mediaeval times for archery products'.

'The fallow seem to know how much they can safely eat when mixed with other browse. In prolonged hard weather, the odd fallow will eat too much and die'. Oddly enough, withered or dying branches of yew are very toxic. A keeper friend recently told me that he has seen several dead fallow beside piles of withered yew. It is a priority for the keepers to remove such dangerous material as soon as possible. Unfortunately, the occasional old yew blown over in a storm or with a damaged branch may not always be reported in time. A professional stalker asserted that fallow are more susceptible to yew poisoning than roe.

DISTRIBUTION MAPS OF THE DIFFERENT DEER SPECIES

Roe Deer

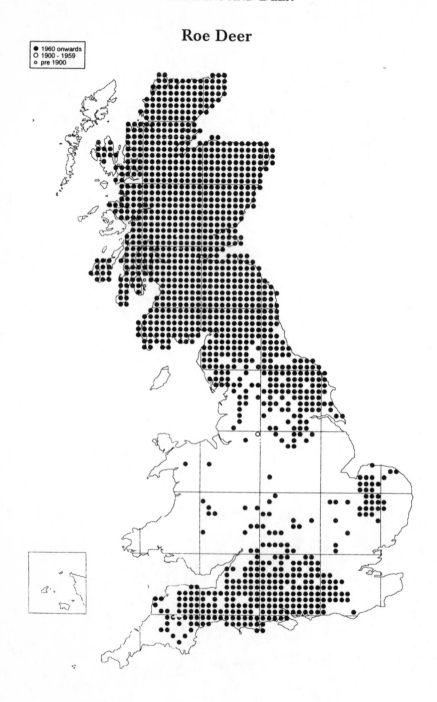

● 1960 onwards
○ 1900 - 1959
∘ pre 1900

Fallow Deer

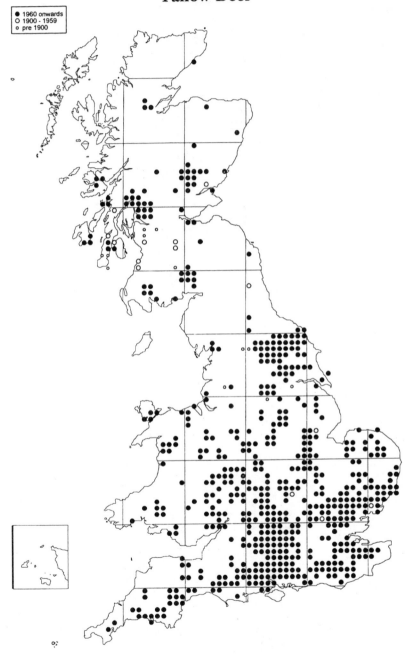

● 1960 onwards
○ 1900 - 1959
o pre 1900

Muntjac

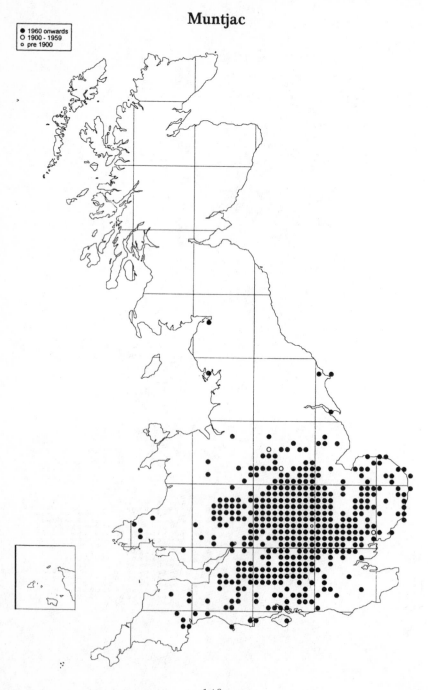

● 1960 onwards
○ 1900 - 1959
∘ pre 1900

Red Deer

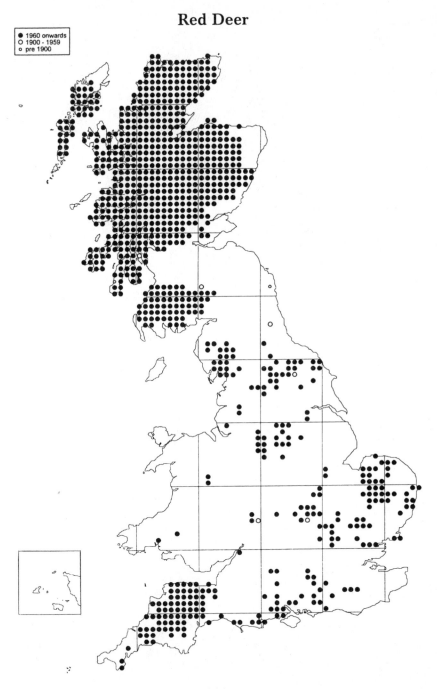

● 1960 onwards
○ 1900 - 1959
∘ pre 1900

Sika

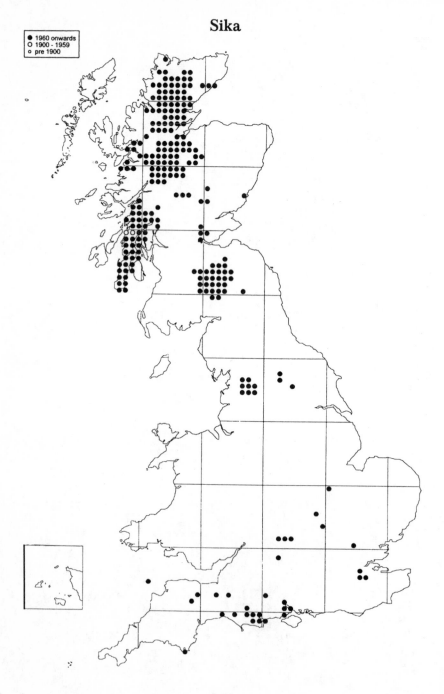